8/2004

To Daniel,

A useful tool . . .

when "leading" the

world . . .

— Karen —

Have you chosen any

colleges yet?

Creativity
FOR
LEADERS

Creativity
FOR
LEADERS

GARY FELLERS

PELICAN PUBLISHING COMPANY
Gretna 1996

Library of Congress Cataloging-in-Publication Data

Fellers, Gary, 1951-
    Creativity for leaders / Gary Fellers.
        p.   cm.
    Includes bibliographical references.
    ISBN 1-56554-162-6 (hc : alk. paper)
    1. Leadership. 2. Creative ability. 3. Creative thinking.
    I. Title.
    HD57.7.F45 1995
    658.4'092—dc20

                                                    95-34489
                                                    CIP

Manufactured in the United States of America

Published by Pelican Publishing Company, Inc.
1101 Monroe Street, Gretna, Louisiana 70053

Contents

Acknowledgments

My wife Pam Fellers listened as I read my work. She spread her natural artistic creativity onto these pages. My mother Jackie Fellers created childhood guidelines that largely made me what I am today. My father George Fellers taught me that some rules can be broken, but not my mother's. (At times coloring outside the lines looked good.)

Nina Kooij and Dr. Milburn Calhoun of Pelican Publishing Company fished this manuscript from the slush pile. Jimmy Peacock edited away the rough edges.

The reviewers below breathed their life experiences into the how-to examples of this book. Their guidance makes the advice profound. I will be forever grateful. My karma included crossing their tracks.

Dr. Joe Tiller—Licensed psychologist
Vicki Hansberger—Roswell, Georgia, school board
Richard Lawson—Quality coordinator
Ernie Hansberger—Consultant
Dan Cherrone—Quality coordinator
Rick Bruce—Quality technician
David Mayberry—Engineer
Dr. Nabil Ibrahim—Professor, Augusta College

Elaine Bruce—Design technician
Col. Larry Keller—Air Force personnel director
Howard Virkler—Industrialist
Drayton Virkler—Student
Ruth Roper—Plant manager
Jenny McAlister—Accountant
Tom Smith—Safety consultant
Lynn Smeltzer—Quality advisor
Dr. Mike McDonald—Professor,
    Georgia Southern University
Mike Gautney—An ordinary guy
Ken Allison—Radio, TV, and newspaper journalist
Pattie Allison—Banker

Introduction

A step-by-step approach that can't miss. The thrust: do this, and here's what happens. The theme: how to untangle and let loose creativity that boredom, fear, or anxiety may have snarled into a web. See how the advice of the mystics applies to help replace knee-jerk struggling with natural leadership—with others and in your own personal battles. Avoid (or rise above) burnout.

I wrote this book for those who hear a faint whisper that life can be different, for those who want for themselves and others a new source of energy, for those who can appreciate—or at least learn to acknowledge—the wisdom illustrated in the story of the guru and the underling:

The follower sat with the guru asking for advice. The elder kept pouring tea, letting the cup overflow onto the floor. When the youngster finally inquired about the odd behavior, the sage said, "Son, you're so full of opinions I can't add anything else. You need first to empty your cup. Then we'll begin."

During fifteen years of hands-on consulting among thousands, I contrasted the successful with the mundane.

Except for a few misguided situations where manipulating career managers used bootlicking to advance, I found the upwardly mobile more creative and innovative. To them, making correct choices came naturally. And most importantly, they had learned to deal with the creativity-destroying fear inherent to the normal workplace. I will show you how.

Have you noticed enthusiastic people who repeatedly unearth creative concepts, seemingly effortlessly, without being bothered by frustrations and anxieties? They live in the same physical world, but pull more inspiration and unique concepts out of the hat, even when a condescending, fear-inducing ogre may be "holding the hat." I show you how to ignite the same motivating fuel, how to follow the advice of the mystics—to initiate magic from your new peace of mind. You'll also benefit from the recommendations of dozens of down-to-earth folks just like you. Every phase of your life will become more fun and productive as creativity replaces overattached and destructive strife.

The most secure and comfortable people I know followed the techniques set forth in this book. They learned to temporarily establish creative presentmindedness, with no guilt from the past or distress for the future. Then they used their uncluttered minds to remove some of the initial stress and burn-out that caused their anxiety.

These creative folks probably learned at an early age to be afraid to fail, or to experiment. But they overcame this outdated fear. They developed ways to let their minds peacefully incubate the issues while they outwardly "took care of demanding business." As they became more creative, enthusiasm sparked in every phase of their lives. They learned that education for living and education for making a living become the same for creative people.

The approach you'll learn applies to circumventing

fear at work, marketing a new product, designing a machine, dealing with a political foe, surviving a libidinous teenager, diagnosing an illness, sculpting an art piece, or catching a fish.

As a consultant, I often visit companies that correctly implemented all the usual organizational fixes—from total quality management to reengineering—yet their employees never "caught the improvement bug." In most cases, the motivated individuals simply did not know how to generate innovative ideas, or else they remained too fearful to try. Luckily, reading this book provides a safe place to start this transition, a way to privately practice "uncluttered presentmindedness."

Unlike many, who stress what's failing, I report what works to increase creativity, what will eventually become a competitive business necessity. Wholeness becomes more difficult as the world grows more complicated.

I urge you to put the principles of this book into practice in your life. Your new accomplishments outside work will dwarf your improved job performance as present-mindedness sets in and anxiety subsides. You'll begin to understand the warnings of the Chinese mystic: "Our thirst for survival in the future makes us incapable of living in the present."

Creativity enhancement yields practical breakthroughs. But for most (and probably you too when you get into it) spiritual energy emerges (or at least something so sublime scientists will never be able to reproduce it in a test tube). Too much magic flows for this phenomenon not to be happening. (Miracles happen, not in opposition to nature, but in conflict with what we know about it.) That's why I enlighten you to the teachings of the mystics—to open your mind to the infinite possibilities. By definition, a mystic is one who, having cast away all ego and attachments, draws insight from higher spiritual powers. Usually such people once struggled with guilt and anxiety. So when they made the conversion, they felt compelled to teach others, often at great personal sacrifice. (If you don't believe things you can't see, you can still benefit from this book. Just ignore the comments about mystics.)

My family doctor told me there exist many types of sickness, but only one kind of good health. I found the same true for creativity. It's an acquired skill, even though, to date, those best at it usually learned by trial-and-error over many years, often oblivious to the process and the gradual enlightenment that accompanies it.

The whole picture comes from several parallel activities: effective time management, mastery of the basics of creativity, stress reduction, and immunization from organizational or everyday barriers. The holistic approach works; nothing else does. Leave out any of these ingredients, and there's less magic. Then your efforts may seem forced, not natural. For a lasting impact, you need all the puzzle parts on the table at the same time in order to get everything into your mind simultaneously. You hold the pieces in your hand. I emphasize the how-to—just follow my instructions. (For skeptical folks, I usually explain why these techniques work.)

One issue has ridden my back for years, like a rabid, clawing raccoon: what if everyone inherently has creative powers, *if* just left alone with their fears erased? (Fear makes cowards of us all.) Not knowing the answer to this question, my intuition forced me to deal extensively with fear at work and anxiety at home when creating this book. In it, I explain how to "escape," even if only momentarily. I also found that for many, including me, the creativity-enhancing approach outlined in this book enabled them to invent an innovative strategy for dealing with the initial root causes of their anxiety. The uncluttered mind sees true issues better. We've all heard there's nothing to fear but fear itself, but this news doesn't help, because it often isn't true. We need more.

The mystics warn that many people remain frightened wanderers. Of most significance: to begin and direct your new journey, remember *the* most important milestone—believing you will become more creative. Skepticism puts out your fire. So loosen up. As Jonas Salk said, "Your intuition will tell your brain where to look next if you just let it work—with confidence it will." The key word here: "confidence."

Believe you can become more creative, and you will.

I restate the major steps in the appendix. Dog-ear those pages and refer to them from time to time until they become "part of you." Then, if you desire, you'll be on your way to becoming a natural leader—of others, of your own destiny. Like most important and mystical forks in the road, the choice is yours.

Too much analysis can drive the romance from anything—a risk I took when writing this book, and a chance you'll take (successfully) as you dissect my recommendations. But when you put the pieces back together, you'll find the total impact of the book to be greater than the sum of its parts: 2 + 2 = 5.

CHAPTER 1

Overview

Knowing where you're going helps you get there. Blind alleys can be stressful. Presentmindedness and its resulting creativity appear when mind chatter dampens, when—among other things—you escape guilt of the past and anxiety for the future.

I devote a chapter to each creativity ingredient, synthesizing as I go. But part of the $2 + 2 = 5$ synergy involves a global view: the thrust of this section. It's easier to piece together a puzzle if you first see the picture.

Unwind, let your thoughts float, and allow this to be fun. Let me help you temporarily fall out of the limited, crowded, everyday mindset into a higher level of thinking. A mystic once said, "Most people exist in psychic sleep—a hypnosis from the anxiety-producing forces of evil." So wake up! At least for a few hours while you read.

In the beginner's brain many possibilities exist. For a moment, loosen up. For now, if necessary, pretend what I say involves the "absolute truth." The power of suggestion will open your mind to get you started. Save your skepticism for later, or maybe never.

Sages and artists for centuries have told us that we come to earth uncritical and creative. Stress, conflict, and anxiety from adult life then crush most of our natural and spontaneous ability. Pablo Picasso stated, "Every child is an artist. The problem becomes how to remain an artist once you grow up" (or how to regain it)—part of the how-to of this book. The innocence of a child's perception contains uninhibited and fruitful insight, breadth of mental association, and an ability to screen the irrelevant: tenfold the capacity of any adult. Children live playfully in the present, with no anxiety about the future or guilt from the past. They have limitless options from their presentmindedness, but they haven't grasped the ways of the world to enable them to put this creativity to practical use. Adults, on the other hand, lose their presentmindedness and spontaneity while grasping the ways of the world.

Before we embrace the latest findings and discover how the less controversial parts of new-spiritualism glue the creativity puzzle together, here's the basic theory: most creativity comes from the subconscious. Everything that has been seen, thought, tasted, experienced, heard, read, or touched combines and remains there, ready to hatch into creative ideas. Both mystics and scientists tell us everything's still there in the subconscious mind. Neurologists have demonstrated this truth by electrically stimulating patients' brains and having them recall in the greatest detail forgotten, trivial events from forty years back. A similar situation often occurs during hypnosis. And it's become almost a trite expression for people brushing death to say, "My whole life passed before me." Also, those who've experienced out-of-body near-death experiences typically recount having every detail of their life played before them. Every thought, action, smell, touch, and feeling came back in three dimensions.

Whether you believe in the spiritual side of near-death experiences remains your choice. But the real (or perceived) replay of these people's entire life still proves one thing: it's all recorded permanently in the subconscious.

Too often the clear insight remains locked inside the subconscious; but occasionally it seeps over into the awareness, when allowed. I'll convince you of the existence and power of the subconscious later. For now:

> **Accept the existence of the mysterious subconscious that incubates all previous experience and facts into creative ideas.**

This concept of the subconscious seems mystical, probably because we don't fully understand all the biochemical processes involved in it. Similarly, we don't have to know how we benefit from oxygen to breathe. The mystics say: "The seed must fall on fertile, not rocky ground." An open mind provides the fertile ground.

Don't see this new approach as gullible, but as practical, eventually leading to profitable decisions and a more peaceful life. Premature, overly analytical thinking or dialogue—hence, schooling—crushes higher-level creative thinking. For centuries mystics, including those in the New Testament, have explained: "By losing our life, we find it." Modern-day, Western thinkers need to cast off some analytical negativism. This open-minded approach allows new concepts a chance to prove themselves. Then creative ideas incubate and flow from the subconscious—unattached to outdated beliefs.

Battling for attention, the brain's opposite component, the overcontrolling conscious mind, excels at analysis and reality-testing a small number of alternatives; hence, attending to work already on the table. (But the short-sighted analytical mind often fails to get the right work onto the table.) Einstein once said, "My analytical mind never discovered anything." The conscious mind can only deal with a half-dozen bits of data, and seldom in parallel. The analytical, conscious mind rarely sees associations of seemingly unrelated concepts, the root of most creativity. However useful at times, the uptight conscious mind can shut down accommodating biochemical processes. This action keeps creativity locked inside the subconscious: *the* problem. Rational thought may carry your luggage and eventually help in finding your way, but that's all it can do. Einstein only developed his theories on the chalkboard; according to him, his ideas came only while shaving or canoeing.

Premature attachment to or overanalysis of an issue often removes the magic. The ego-infested conscious mind dries up your creative juices when it gets easily and prematurely distracted: by bosses, by fears, by overattachment, by fictitious deadlines, by your spouse, by your own expectations for yourself, by struggles to impress others, and by numerous other day-ruiners and creativity-destroyers. A large part of becoming more creative will involve developing ways to overpower judgmental thoughts and creativity blockers, often forever, sometimes only momentarily. Then utilizing the tools you're about to learn, unattached creativity will solve the problem at hand. Always. When unattached, the answers invariably come.

When allowed, the creative subconscious mind incubates twenty-four hours a day: categorizing, associating dissimilar phenomena, correlating, sorting, comparing, and storing an almost infinite quantity of insight. Dreams flow from the subconscious. Remembering someone's name in a flash when not thinking about it—after a stretch of useless struggling—comes from the subconscious. When looking for a lost item, surrendering and asking a friend for help often releases the subconscious to reveal its whereabouts. The brilliance of your subconscious will emerge more often when you learn to let it. At times, if you prefer, you can release your untapped potential while behaving playfully and fearlessly in the privacy of your own mind. Rigid-thinking associates do not have to get involved until invited.

The natural balancing forces of Zen apply here. A life in equilibrium only comes when the quiet intuition of the subconscious (the yen) balances the unrelenting analytical judgments and ego attachments of the verbal conscious mind (the yang). Most experts refer to the creative part of the psyche as the right brain, and the analytical, judgmental portion as the left (hence, left-brained tax lawyers and right-brained poets). The latest investigations support this left-analytical, right-intuitive model. Yale scientists Sally and Bennett Shaywitz reinforced the brain duality theory by electronically monitoring male and female brains during talking, an activity previously believed to be a pure left-brain activity. When repeating benign nonsense words, only the verbal left side of the men's brains operated, as expected. But the women used both the verbal left and intuitive-emotional right sides of their brains to process language. Also, other recent studies showed men having fewer fibers connecting the two brain hemispheres. All this work confirms folk wisdom: the idea that women express emotions better than men, the concept of woman's intuition, the fact that most men can "pull down the hatches" (isolate the left brain from emotions) better to do mathematical calculations. Is the average woman inherently more creative (intuitive) than the average man? Probably. Can men benefit as much as women from this book? Definitely. With fewer fibers connecting the two brain hemispheres, we men have to work harder to pull our soft intuitive powers into the open. (When listening to me read the first draft of this book, my wife interjected, "That means: shut up and listen!" Could she have been talking about me?)

As you read, you'll learn how to solve the yen-yang struggle and how to resolve the similar left-brain, right-brain conflict. It takes both brain hemispheres, in balance, to earn a living the creative way.

In seminars, I use a toy treasure chest as a model for the subconscious and its wealth of insight and knowledge. For at least sixty seconds—eyes closed—picture in your mind your subconscious as a treasure chest, with gold nuggets of creativity overflowing. (Don't cheat on the time!)

You'll learn to have fun adding more creativity-inducing material to your treasure chest—in some cases, making up for years with your new and efficient approach to richness and diversity. I call this feeding of the subconscious the "enrichment"—placing more nuggets into the chest.

Putting more rich experiences into the treasure chest—enriching the subconscious—covers about twenty percent of the effort. Also, along with providing explicit steps to follow to bring forth your creativity, I devote entire chapters to taming the inhibitors and fears of the enthusiasm-stomping conscious mind. (I will cover this process in more detail later.)

The heaviest weight holding down that treasure chest lid is the question: "What will everybody think?" You can't go through life unfocused and foolishly flamboyant; but the treasure chest stays closed when you are preoccupied with boss-watching, trying to appease your bellyaching spouse, or impressing others. You can become a prisoner to others' expectations. On the other hand, creative ideas can flow from the subconscious and fuse with the issue at hand only when you learn to quiet the "Voice **Of** Judgment," or VOJ. The VOJ criticizes, blames, assigns guilt, tries to impress, and puts down. All of these are negative actions primarily related to ego. Here's an example: when considering leaving a dead-end job, one with a boss of anti-Christ meanness, your VOJ keeps the treasure chest closed by shouting into the pit of your stomach: "Quitters never win; don't walk away from your problems. What will people think? Better safe than sorry." All this advice remains good at times, but maybe not for this quicksand. Something I once heard stuck in my subconscious: "No problem's so big we can't run away from it." With no security fears, that might be the advice to follow with the punishing boss.

The mystics teach that most people struggle with two conflicting selves: the inner "true" self and the outer "false" self. The "false" self and the VOJ closely personify the same destructive force, which must be identified and locked away so wholeness can be achieved. The mystics say that the "false" self and its guilt cannot be changed, so don't waste time trying. But the evil force must be identified and imprisoned, which involves a large part of what you will learn from this book. Incarcerating your VOJ enables you to bring home your scattered mind. (You can let the VOJ out during those rare times you need to be judgmental.)

More positively, religious leaders and other mystics often teach that "the kingdom of heaven exists within you." Your palace becomes your subconscious when you are untainted with guilt or fear, when your creativity flows because of your unattachment, and when you have no anxiety about failure.

Improvements coming from this kind of state of mind usually enable everyone to win; some do not have to suffer for others to benefit. But those not in touch with their subconscious often act from ego-based drives or fears, and frequently back-stab associates or waste energy boss-watching. They usually never become creative because they suffer subconscious guilt. They have some sort of soul even if they don't know it. (Forward the name and address of these lower-level thinkers in your life. I'll send them a tactful note recommending this book.)

Guilt lingers as the worst treasure-chest closer. We all need our conscience; but for some people, the conscience remains unrealistic and doesn't prevent sin, it just keeps them from enjoying it. The creative subconscious shuts down from guilt. The yin and yang don't balance; the person withers.

After becoming and remaining unattached and non-judgmental—enabling your subconscious to help generate lots of ideas—you can later analyze and criticize to your heart's content. This becomes a separate, distinct, and subsequent step of the creative process: the *verification stage,* a time when you finally subject your intuitive gut feelings to reality and compare all the alternatives. You'll learn how to let multiple options freely flow out onto the table. No risk lurks because you can keep your thoughts to yourself at first and then compare and rip them apart later during your separate verification stage. Ultimately you'll bring one brilliant idea out into the open for implementation, one you might have missed if you had remained uptight.

Similarly, you've probably noticed in business meetings how people, particularly "specialists," dwell on why something *can't* be done. (They want the boss to know they spotted the hurdles everyone else has missed.) When you learn to be creative, you'll look for reasons why things *can* be done and will try to create wide-angled alternatives. By playing angel's advocate, you'll delay the can't-do attitude until the final verification stage, which may be the next day. There will be plenty of devil's advocates around when you need them later. So save the criticism for now. Premature negativism shuts down the rich creative process. (It's a biochemical thing.)

Pertaining to business management, the quality revolution of the 1980s seemed to overly emphasize managing with quantifiable facts and data, without gut feelings. Formal schooling has always overemphasized mind-strangling analytical skills at the expense of openmindedness. I'm not taking sides on quantitative procedures versus intuition. Both can be used simultaneously: to blend facts, data, and "hunches." Mastering change requires both: "soft" creative powers followed by "hard" analytic skills. Enhancing individual creativity provides the last piece of the quality-improvement puzzle, the one most of us missed during the last decade.

Another hang-up we need to overcome: accepting too quickly the first solution coming to mind—called "satisficing" by academics. Our teachers unintentionally taught us, "Get an answer and move on to the next question." We seldom learned something more important: how to generate more questions. Our primitive impulse (and laziness) seeks the quickest path for reducing fear and danger, or getting the issue "off our desk."

In a business setting the first, but usually not the best, solution often surges from political apprehension. When generating creative ideas in the privacy of your own mind, go to the opposite extreme to become temporarily unattached. Ask yourself, "What rules can I break, who can I tick off, and what can I do to aggravate the guy in the corner office the most?" At times, these questions lead to important root causes. Of course, you can later cull the mean alternatives that would get you fired or do unjust harm to someone else.

So far much of what you've read exists in mainstream creativity research and will be expanded in the next chapter. Now let's get to some new parts to launch the 2 + 2 = 5 synergy. To enrich your subconscious, you'll need free moments. I sandwich many time-management techniques in with the meat of this book. But not the fanatical, time-consuming rituals like keeping a minute-by-minute log of where your time went. (We've all been told to try this practice, but how many of us actually did?) I stick to techniques I use. For example: how to spend five minutes when stuck waiting; how to schedule "worry time" in order to get on with the work at hand without being anxious about what you aren't doing.

I will discuss the tricks of the creativity trade such as: keeping a bright-ideas note pad or recorder handy to sweep up anything that seeps from the subconscious, before it vanishes in front of your eyes. Creativity inspires with its promise of something, where just a moment ago there was nothing. It can slip away.

The time-management ideas reduce stress. Anxiety closes the subconscious outlet and produces the primitive fight-or-flight response. We want to replace this response with the stay-and-play response. Today's challenges require calm persistence and creative problem-solving. We self-invoke most anxiety, or unnecessarily allow it to overcome us. As Shakespeare said, "Things are neither good nor bad, but thinking makes it so." This is true most of the time; yet at times it isn't. Learning to quiet your near-useless, guilt-invoking voice of judgment (VOJ) will help you follow Shakespeare's advice, not twenty four-hours a day, but for your creative moments.

Dr. Wayne Dyer calls the VOJ our "erroneous zones"—self-defeating behavior patterns that rob our happiness. Most of them developed as mental escapes early in life, when our parents and teachers limited our behavioral and thought options. Typical erroneous zones: constantly seeking approval, giving in to guilt, nagging a loved one for affection. We often cling to these habits to feel psychologically safe and secure, at the expense of our personal growth. Someone estimated that we think sixty thousand thoughts each day, much of this mental activity being self-destructive mind chatter. A mystic once said, "A mind too active is no mind at all." Just below this constant stream of babble remains a space in the mind of creative calm and quiet. The suggestions of this book will help you attain presentmindedness as you overcome mental scurry.

The present, free from guilt and anxiety, remains the only moment you can totally control. When you learn to initiate presentmindedness, your friends will see your glow. Your radiant clarity of awareness will rub off on some of them. But if the stoic numskulls at work cannot accept delightful free spirits, there's no reason why you can't practice my advice in the seclusion of your own mind.

"Surrender" and believe you can be more creative, and you will be. Your subconscious will help you work out a way.

CHAPTER 2

Enrichment

You can have fun making up for years of mental stagnation in several months with no down side. Your I.Q. increases as you rise above your present level of thinking—your sticks-and-stones image of the world.

When presentminded (unattached, non-judgmental, unpretentious), the higher self delves into the subconscious and retrieves bits of information. These tidbits fuse with new facts into creative discoveries. But casting a net into an empty pond yields nothing. The subconscious "enrichment" supplies the fish.

Most creativity experts call the enrichment phase the "preparation." To me, this word sounds too stoic and reeks of unpleasant struggling. If approached properly, and if equated to your life purpose, the enrichment will be easy, enjoyable, and effortless. (More on life purposes follows.)

The subconscious' remarkable ability to generate ideas works like a kaleidoscope's capacity to produce patterns— restrained only by the number and variety of colored fragments. Creative people fill knowledge gaps by absorbing interesting facts like a sponge does water. Equally important, they remain calm when facing what they don't yet know. They view things yet to be learned as one of the many exciting reasons for existing.

A long-term biological change comes with learning. I read somewhere that scientists at the UCLA Brain Research Institute studied the brains of twenty dead patients, half educated and curious learners, half not. (To find out which was which, I suppose they interviewed friends or relatives.) The learned ones had significantly longer dendrites, the branch-like parts of nerve cells that convey information. The analysis of Einstein's brain showed the same pattern.

The most profound part of the creativity process involves surrendering—cleansing away the ego and other distractions. Without guilt from the past or anxiety about the future, presentmindedness lets your subconscious' wisdom seep into your awareness. Yet the total process encompasses more. The long-haired guru in India under the same tree for thirty years probably remains in touch with his subconscious. But I doubt he has the technical enrichment to help with your complicated opportunities.

Unlike children or the gray-bearded guru, most of us lack the uncluttered and calm mind to draw on our subconscious whenever we need its bounty. We want this peace of mind and the better relationship to time promised by the mystics. But we also want these close encounters with our near-mystical subconscious to produce creative solutions to our everyday problems: to put bread on the table or money in the bank, or to develop a way to deal with the guy down the hall who's trying to "stab us in the back." So we practical souls begin with the lifelong process of "enriching" the subconscious, feeding it interesting facts and experiences. By applying the principles of this book, you'll have fun speeding up this process and will make up for years in a few weeks.

Mystics say that homo sapiens come to earth as spiritual beings looking for a human experience—mostly to learn and to help others—constrained only by the forces of evil with guilt and fear as their weapons. They say humans take this learning back to the spiritual world, and then sort it all out. If true, the enrichment (learning) may even fulfill holy covenants.

You'll have fun, but "get dirty" becoming creative. As the Chinese proverb reveals: "He who waits for roast duck to fly into mouth must wait very, very long time." As an example, entrepreneurs reportedly use the intuitive (creative) process to "smell" money, as if born with this capability. These tycoons have gleaned an almost infinite database of facts and experiences—sometimes unconsciously, but usually through conscious brain enrichment. They talk to people, they discover unfulfilled needs, they learn how to arrange financing, they take nothing for granted, they learn from mistakes (especially those of others), they read. Most importantly, they've learned how to act and when; they know the right time to gather facts and feelings into money-making ideas. Entrepreneurs tell me: "Experience is not what happens to you; it's what you do with what happens."

Couch potatoes will not benefit much from this book. Routine dulls the eye and ear; repetition and familiarity fog the capacity for astonishment—the "whack" of excitement needed to become more creative. Boredom, anxiety, and fear close the subconscious down tight for twenty-four hours. Sensory "whacks" open it back up for several days by starting the emphatic biochemical processes going again.

With the goal of having more fun, create a life plan to "enrich" your subconscious.

The remainder of this chapter may read like a laundry list of a free-wheeling author's favorite pastimes, but it runs deeper. I reviewed the current creativity literature well and talked to hundreds of creative people. Hidden magic hides in this list of items, or similar activities. If your brain remains entrapped, the following suggestions, along with a few of your own, will "trick your brain back" into becoming more creative.

Read Widely

I have known few creative people who do not read. Varied experiences enrich the subconscious, but none of us can live long enough to personally encounter all we want or need to know.

Your best creativity generally comes in your own area of expertise, so routinely read the relevant sections of one or more technical trade journals with felt-tip pen in hand. (If this bores you, change specialties, and don't feel guilty.) Underline, dog-ear, and keep a notebook of assorted facts and ideas you may want to try someday. You probably learned in school that by the time you write something, you know it; but there's more. I keep these notebooks forever; my subconscious knows this fact, so I'm relieved of the stress of fearing I may forget something important.

Keep a folder of torn-out articles by the toilet and take them on planes. Never use prime eight-to-five hours or family time for wide-angled reading; it will cause too much guilt. (I stay several months behind in my reading and don't worry about it.) If the stack starts looking too thick, put it out of sight to prevent stress. Don't take the folder on vacations either; carry along only your pocket note pad to catch elusive insights when they spring from your subconscious.

Reading business publications keeps you apprised of buzzwords and trends; reading fiction keeps you balanced. A novel or two a year may suffice. And by all means, absorb some books on the philosophy of Edwards Deming. This visionary captured ten thousand years of wisdom in his theories and explained about ninety percent of why things go wrong in business management, and why we remain so stressed. He explained why there are almost no natural leaders on the job, and how this trend can be reversed. (See REFERENCES, Fellers, *Why Things Go Wrong.*)

Visualizing the desired qualitative outcome will become an important part of your creative process. But as it pertains to business, Deming clearly showed what mystics explained centuries ago: overconcern with numerical results usually becomes a major torture to man, when trying to use wide-angled vision looking for a better way. For example, often no answer exists to such questions by management as: "Why did we sell only 997 units, when our goal was a thousand? You failed to meet your objectives! YOU DON'T GET YOUR BONUS." A certain amount of uncontrollable variability lingers in the marketplace. These numerically based questions often lead to the pitfall that causes failure—employees spending potentially productive hours putting on false appearances, and losing their spontaneity (creativity) while fibbing. It's estimated that fifty percent of the work done in commerce exists to make things look like something they're not. The process *is* the game, not the measurement of after-the-fact, short-term financial results—the way it's taught in most business schools. (That's like driving a car only looking in the rearview mirror.) Deming also brought the creativity-destroying problem of job fear into sharp focus. As Ian Fleming said, "Fear is the dividend paid to disaster before it happens." (For more on fear, see REFERENCES, Fellers, *Why Things Go Wrong*.)

About once a year a good crossover book hits the shelves (see REFERENCES). These make good reads for creativity. They force the mind to associate unrelated concepts, a big part of innovation. Also, study one of the mini-MBA books. Administrators and bureaucrats through their paperwork and procedures often seem to be trying to kill creative passion once and for all! They erroneously think that more rules and laws will make sure nothing *ever* goes wrong. And they are willing to let their companies waste money doing so. Like the Department of Defense when reconciling travel expense vouchers, they are willing to spend half as much on the paperwork to safeguard against cheating as on the travel itself (actual statistic!). If you understand the bureaucrats' craft, you can help them avoid this trap.

Practice Intense Observation

Daily drudgery numbs. Sometimes we further immerse ourselves in trivia to anesthetize ourselves from boredom or stress. The unattended mind lazily seeks the path of least resistance.

Pick moments to reverse this trend. Practice intense observation, just for the sake of doing it. Several times a day, for five minutes, become immersed in the moment while observing rain or children playing. I've heard these sublime periods called "nevertime," a few minutes to soften and expand work's hard edge. You often need to relax most when you don't have time.

When you do this exercise, try to get several of the five senses involved. I've noticed that creative people look, touch, taste, hear, and smell, when uptight people usually only glance with bloodshot eyes.

Remain curious with this intense observation, and don't worry about how to use what you learn. Make no judgments or analyses, but do pay attention. (A wandering mind may fail to find its way home.)

You'll need to practice to get into the presentness of this exercise, but it will come. And when it does, notice how the simple concept of unattached, penetrating observation increases your mental energy and enhances your curiosity, a necessity for creativity. Within the next month and about twice a year (forever), take an entire conscious-of-being-conscious day. Put it on your calendar now. Keep your outer self—the VOJ—quiet for the entire day. See how the enlightenment it brings wipes away the cobwebs as you unjudgingly observe.

Never walk around in a trance: hear the birds, keep your eyes on the ball, and smell the blossoms. The mystics tell us that getting lost in thought blocks moving into higher levels of thinking. Dreaming as a form of visualization may be good; goofy-expressioned gazing at a wall isn't. If the last hour wasn't informative or fun—or a contribution to your presentmindedness—you wasted it.

Also practice being an observer of yourself. "Psyche out" and pretend you're someone else watching over your shoulder. Notice your mannerisms and speech. You may see the absurdity of it all.

Consider yourself as an actor playing some pretentious part. Eventually the costume will fall away and the inner self will emerge. Riches of all sorts will follow, often through mysterious and yet-unthought-of ways. As the mystics tell us, until we discover our creative selves, we all roleplay ego-centered scripts. The overattachment causes us to burn out. "A life unexamined is not worth living," Plato said.

Avoid Articulate Incompetents

Articulate incompetents know everything but understand nothing. They can sound just wonderful, even when they know zilch about the subject. The Tibetan saying, "If you are too clever, you could miss the point entirely," applies here. Students from business schools emphasizing case studies can fall into this trap if the professor grades on the quantity of classroom participation.

Articulate incompetents dawdled around even in Lincoln's day. He referred to them as guys who could compress the largest amount of words into the smallest thought. Or could stay longer in an hour than others could in a week.

A problem never existed, however complicated, that articulate incompetents could not make more devastating by causing it to look too simple. Their oversimplification can fool the often gullible subconscious. Over the long haul only your intuition will protect you from such guys— that is, assuming you don't let them pre-program your treasure chest. When an articulate incompetent makes the mistake of bringing a hazy concept into too sharp a focus, your impressionable subconscious may mistakenly tuck this generalization away "as is." Adult creative minds usually survive any kind of bad training, but overgeneralizers can prevent you from becoming creative if they get to you too soon.

Articulate incompetents have well-developed left brains (where verbal skills come from), but underdeveloped right brains (where the softer intuitive powers come from).

Guys scare me who have everything all worked out—an articulate explanation for everything. I've learned that no questions, no creativity; all avenues of new thought closed; brain cells dying by the millions behind hollow eyeballs attached to a glib tongue. Along similar lines, when looking for extraordinary creative ideas, I've learned to avoid those whose hair never gets messed up, or guys who polish their shoes just before meetings with the boss. Egotism hammers down creativity, so these people must present a facade of some sort to maintain a false image of innovativeness. Trivial matters become important to lower-level minds. Break this trend if it applies to you.

If you're an articulate incompetent, stop it! Right now. You can tell if you're one: does the crowd start to thin when you walk up or begin to talk? If you fear being lonely, don't try to always be right, or to know it all, or to get the last word, or to top every story told to you with a bigger tale. In fewer words: shut up!

Do "Different Stuff"

Variety seasons. Live, live, and then live some more. Seek that wide-eyed look of a kid in the zoo for the first time. New surroundings "whack" the system, releasing a host of creativity-enhancing biochemicals to the brain—glycogen for one. Remember falling passionately in love? Weren't the flowers more colorful and the sky bluer? Remember how trivial irritants bothered you less? A cocktail of natural chemicals triggered by the subconscious caused this state of mind. By following my recommendations, you'll learn to bring them back into play at will.

The drop-jawed innocence of new experiences makes

you absorb everything and reverses the "tricks" that fear and job anxiety have played on your brain, tying it and your stomach into knots. Novelty forces your subconscious to work double time, quickly correlating and contrasting new input with past experiences, associating it all. The 2 + 2 = 5 synergy may even form a new connection in your subconscious, one that you aren't aware of at the moment. The treasure chest may open later when needed.

Einstein floated in a canoe, Hemingway often worked standing in the nude, Alex Haley wrote only while riding in merchant marine ships, and the list goes on. Creative people "whack" their brains often. Try these creativity-enhancing ideas:

1. Dine with old friends in new places.
2. Every month, scheduled on your calendar, do something greatly different. Go to a rodeo, ice skate, hike a mountain, ride a horse.
3. Experiment with a new mode of travel—a bus or train to a routine place will do.
4. Walk a route you've driven for years. Notice what you've been missing.
5. Talk to an old person on a park bench. Observe what a different perspective someone with absolutely no "agendas" has. This shock will "whack" the old noggin.
6. Go to a concert or live theater.
7. Attend the opera. (But sit near an exit on the aisle.)
8. Take a brisk twenty-minute walk every day to clear your mind. (Do it within a half-hour after dinner and burn twice the calories.)
9. Take eight to ten five-minute brain-balancing breaks a day. Do something sensory and different. Stand if you usually sit; enjoy colorful flowers if you study data summaries all day; move around.

10. Start a new hobby. Becoming an imperfect beginner at something starts the creativity-enhancing biochemical processes churning. The brain just works that way—as a survival tool, I suppose.

Variety sparks a continued need for diversity. You'll get hooked on the novelty, and your friends will see the new gleam in your eyes. The time you spend exploring will be returned fivefold in the form of increased enthusiasm and efficiency. And it won't take as much time as you may think. The more "different" your activities, the more creativity-enhancing wonder you'll reap for a small time investment.

Here's another "whack" that also reduces anxiety: many successful people approach a new issue by inoculating their subconscious with the "worst that could happen." They tuck away a tentative plan of action for the potential disaster, just in case. This sounds pessimistic, a creativity killer, but it isn't. Having enriched their subconscious by attending to "the worst," they can move on presentmindedly to develop lots of creative alternatives. By the way, for me the "worst" never happened because my open-minded attitude always yielded many alternatives, at least one fitting my predicament or opportunity. I'll admit, occasionally the subconscious met my needs in ways that seemed mysterious to me at the moment. But I understood later.

A few more suggestions: you have no friends like old friends. But you may find some new ones different from you to be invigorating: an architect if you're an accountant, a plumber if you're a teacher. This exposure to new ideas will enrich and stimulate your subconscious. The magic happens as your world opens. Maybe you'll get lucky and they'll tell you when you're becoming a total fool, or killing yourself. I'm an engineer, an MBA, and a statistician. My friends are musicians, philosophers, machinists, and repair people, with a psychologist and teacher or two thrown in for good measure and variety; no MBA-engineers, like me.

Spontaneity's great, but plan part of your weekends by Wednesday night—and schedule big adventures. If you wait until the day comes, it's too tempting to just watch the tube, clean out the garage, or weed a flower bed. Maybe set aside one weekend out of three for home chores. Keep a running list of these rude distractions and another for supplies and tools. Then forget them until the designated "sweat day." (I warn the kids and wife to stay away from bad-mood daddy on these terrible days; it's not a good time to ask for a moped or an opinion on world affairs.)

Most creativity starts with questions, usually undirected, dumb questions. Many of the lessons of growing up—such as: seen, but not heard—discouraged questions for the sake of questions. Creative people learn to overcome this mind-closing and ask many dumb questions (even if only to themselves). Who knows what you may learn that will be a part of a creative idea? Taking the dumb-question recommendation one step further: problems remaining persistently unsolvable for great minds usually become suspect as questions asked the wrong way. Einstein said, "The important thing is not to stop questioning." Those who knew him best often spoke of his ability to ask questions in ways that seemed unique or odd to lesser minds. As you will do if you are willing, he lost his destructive ego attachment and wasn't afraid to probe. He became smarter and more creative by the day.

For problems that won't yield, pretend *everything* you're doing (that's related) is unsuitable, that you need to reengineer from scratch. This means forgetting all rules and procedures. If no "givens" exist, what will you do? Of course, you don't change "everything," but by temporarily removing attachment to all policies and beliefs, you can open your creativity. Here's another related dumb question to apply to procedures and bureaucratic paper shuffling at work: "Why do we even do this at all?" Sometimes the creative solution involves not "how to do this a different way," but "Let's quit this."

About fifty percent of the questions posed in meetings and classrooms are asked to demonstrate what people already know or to feed some other personal agenda, not to enrich discussion. It may be some time before this roleplaying subsides. So maybe you won't present dumb questions in business meetings. Ask friendly strangers and craftsmen. They love to talk.

Sharpening your creativity involves some pleasant exertion as you enrich your subconscious. As Michelangelo once said, "If people knew how hard I worked to get my mastery, it wouldn't seem so wonderful at all." Nothing's free. Genius comes to a talented person who does his homework.

Enriching the subconscious involves changing your lifestyle—in the direction of more fun. But don't choke on my recommendations; you can start implementing them while you're jumping right into the how-to ideas of later chapters. When comparing these get-down-and-dirty recommendations with the more philosophical suggestions of later chapters, your encouragement may hang in the words of Einstein, "Imagination is more important than information."

Enriching the subconscious only sparks the beginning. Knowledge without insight is like a dog in a classroom.

Keep an open mind and your insight will come as you turn the pages.

———————————————————

Your assignment: plan this weekend around something different and take all steps to make your plans a reality. Decide with your family tonight.

CHAPTER 3

Incubation

Discover how to turn on the calm mind when you need inno-
vative ideas. The mysterious subconscious does the hard
work—requiring little draining effort to distract from your
pressing short-term objectives.

You know how to enrich your subconscious, so now let's learn to incubate. Only in quiet waters do objects mirror themselves without distortion. Only in a calm mind exists a true perception of the world (or so I read somewhere). The essence of this chapter involves enhancing your incubation—the quiet, internal workings of your mysterious subconscious.

This exercise will take practice. A mystic once compared modern-day man to the panicky passenger on a reliable ocean liner. He races furiously toward the bow of the ship not realizing that he gets to port at the same time as the others. (And all passengers exit the middle of the vessel.) Similarly, some managers look like idiots with a German shepherd on a leash trying to herd cats, not knowing they'd follow if he'd lose the dog and open a can of tuna.

The creative insight coming from the subconscious can

be many times greater than what is put into it. Ideas incubate from the subconscious' ability to correlate, combine, associate, ignore, and categorize. Thinkers for ages have sought to understand its mysticism.

Our subconscious mind heals us, yet lets us get sick when something tells it, "What's the use?"; and when allowed, enchantingly it incubates everything we've experienced.

Medical literature contains many studies proving that through the power of suggestion to the subconscious, our thoughts control many bodily functions affecting our state of mind, creativity, and health—from white blood count, to the production of endorphins (the body's natural high), to the output of neuropeptides to direct the immune system. On the other hand, our conscious mind, our ego, overattachment, stress, and our reaction to other people, hinder the incubation process.

I promise not to let this book float off into the cosmos; however, I will state in passing that there's some evidence that everything in the universe links through our collective subconscious minds. (Our cells possibly even remember our ancestors.) Here's an example: the mere fact something has been done—somewhere on earth—seems to make others in faraway places more likely to accomplish the same feat. From sports, we all know the story about the four-minute-mile block and how once someone broke the barrier, people worldwide began to do it in droves. Their subconscious minds told them, "Go ahead. Now you know: it can be done." And there's more. Cases exist where breaking a barrier had a similar effect even when people couldn't have known that the boundary had been broken. People's subconscious minds knew. Somehow, they knew. "Connected" power exists in our subconscious beyond what rational analysis can verify. The mystics call this source of knowledge the "cosmos." The great Swiss scientist and psychiatrist Carl Jung remained one of the more prominent thinkers of our time who believed all minds exist in unconscious contact with each other on a deep level. (I could prove this theory about as easily as I could disprove it.) Most ultra-creative, great minds accept that this hypothesis could be true. It will aid presentmindedness to keep the option open.

Now back to what can be proven, or at least talked about from practical experience. Incubation can be enhanced, or at least distractions can be prevented. Some of the new experiences listed in the previous chapter will help. Fresh or even bizarre encounters force the subconscious to start its computer—trying to figure out what the heck's going on. Then new correlations and associations percolate to get tucked away for later use. It takes only about one-tenth of a second to put a wrinkle in the subconscious, and you may not even realize you've done it.

Trust and remain patient. The subconscious always responds, but usually at its own pace, and only when you learn to let go. The treasure chest (enriched subconscious) may close if you hurry it. One reason procrastinators seldom become creative: deadlines sneak up on them. Incubation takes time, so innovative people plan and plant seeds early. The incubation process fertilizes the seed—with no conscious effort. It's free.

Patiently trust that answers will come.

Occasionally, testosterone-driven knee-jerkers falsely accuse us creative folks of procrastinating, because we try to wait as long as possible on the intuitive powers of the subconscious. Patiently pausing for issues to incubate differs from goofing off—it's perhaps just the opposite. You can incubate one issue along with others, while you outwardly work on something else. The subconscious incubates dozens of topics in parallel. Creative folks learn to remain unstressed (as you will) by having only one active issue "on the desk," although they may be incubating many. In later chapters I refer to this as "creatively attending to the work at hand."

For big, tough issues, try to plan ahead days, weeks, or even months (in an unstressful way). Introduce topics and problems to your subconscious long before due dates. At the outset, drench yourself and your subconscious with all the facts you can muster (especially take into account others' facial expressions and your queasy feelings). Don't question their relevance too strongly or analyze their significance too heavily—not yet anyway. Your subconscious blends this new database with everything else you've experienced—and maybe even what your great-great-grandfather thought—if you don't let the evil forces of judgment, overattachment, and fear intervene.

Then on your calendar make two notes, on different dates: 1) when to revisit the thought processes, and 2) when to collect everything to make decisions, write speeches, or compare alternatives—in a phrase, when to do the outward, conscious work.

My system always works; it never has failed. I tell my subconscious to get to work. I give it long-term deadlines but ample time. I surrender and trust. I expect, and it delivers wide-angled alternatives. Writing dates on my calendar eliminates the stress and fear of possibly forgetting.

Avoid conscious analysis and judgment during this incubation period. The uptight conscious brain may force the subconscious to hurry or to "face the facts." Anxiety-based, politically inspired, ego-driven, or guilt-laden emotions shut down part of the subconscious. (Fear and anger, we know, reduce the body's level of energizing endorphins.) We'll have time for reality checks later during the verification stage of the creative process. So float above it all at this point. Don't worry yet about what the sourpuss down the hall will think. (Master the techniques of this book and you'll become immune to energy-draining ogres. Or better, you'll eliminate them from your life—with a creative flair.)

The major reason my clients need me to help them unwind and to solve their problems: they can't generate creative lists of options from worrying too soon about the problems of implementation. I tell them: "Look for reasons why we *can* do things and why we *will* succeed. We'll eventually get some nitpickers to alert us of the problems, but only near the end of our investigation." Remaining uptight and overattached about something causes a self-fulfilling prophecy: the problem prevents the discovery of the solution to the problem. Letting go—knowing all along that you'll subsequently reality check all the options—will help you presentmindedly get many alternatives onto the table.

For at least thirty seconds, always visualize your desired outcome—in the broadest sense—leaving the particulars to your subconscious. (Never put a number on your desire.) Incubation begins helping you to discover what's missing or to synthesize what's already there. For example, I would never tell my subconscious to produce a best-selling book. I will, however, prompt my subconscious to lead me to the experiences, energy, motivation, and health to create a best-seller. The magic goes to work.

Trigger the subconscious by "visualizing" the desired outcome—in general terms.

Several times this week visualize what it would be like to have no fear or anxiety, not to be at the mercy of anything in your world. Experience the feeling for at least sixty seconds. Once your subconscious gets a taste of this wonderful sensation, the incubation starts. Eventually you'll gain the experiences and insights you need to get there. Or you'll discover that there's enough payback to make the anxiety worthwhile. Even this experience will give you peace.

During the incubation interval, you may unintentionally unearth a few new facts; if so, let your subconscious tuck them away. And certainly do a bunch of listening (great incubation fertilizer—especially when done across several layers in the hierarchy or different age groups). But be careful while your subconscious incubates not to get drawn prematurely into detailed analysis or argumentative dialogue. That kind of activity comes later during the verification process in which you test against reality the intuition's wealth of alternatives.

For the unenlightened, the contaminated "outer" self (VOJ) the mystics speak of remains frightened by creativity. From the inborn survival impulse—not to mention ego battles—talking with others can hammer away innovativeness. It's the primitive and inherently scared VOJ that scans the creative meadow outside the cave for beasts and dangers. Others will remind you of this fact. You'll learn to reveal early alternatives and hunches to only a select few higher-level thinkers.

At work always start and end creative meetings by saying, "We will not reach all the decisions today, and will not make anything final until we sleep on it." This approach works especially well with brainstorming sessions in which non-threatening groups enumerate the first thoughts coming to mind. Brainstorming and documenting "first" thoughts takes discipline; "second," and "third" thoughts often come from the VOJ with the intent of killing creativity. I once heard a mystic say, "God speaks first. Then the devil tries to butt in and get the last word." (This rascal—which some say only exists in the mind—works mostly through guilt, overjudgment, and fear.) Let the team members come back later to compare and analyze brainstormed alternatives.

When I'm with clients and find them in a reflective mood, I ask the question, "What would your one wish for work be if you could wave a magic wand and have it come true?" I give them about twenty seconds to respond. The answer to this question often bypasses stress and politics and reveals to me what's incubating in their subconscious. We usually achieve their wishes (unless these wishes are politically motivated, ego-driven, or fear-based).

You can't effectively use the by-the-book creative process for got-to-have-an-answer-by-the-end-of-the-day emergencies. However, I don't think I need to insult your intelligence by giving you a dozen examples of situations I've seen in which creative prevention would have thwarted emergencies.

Help others incubate for you. Plant your seeds. For example, send out memos in advance of meetings to pique the subconscious of attendees. This early notice will spark their interest to get the incubation processes started, and it may get lady luck on your side.

Talk to thriving superstars; they constantly refer to their "breaks." Fortune seems to favor well-prepared people. Magic usually occurs when you follow your subconscious to be at the right place at the right time, with all bases covered—especially when you also have others behind the scenes moving in the same direction. Most troubled people and managers fail to acknowledge the gentle nudges of the subconscious, and/or they treat others in such a way that nothing good happens when they're not around.

Often this happens because they have no one incubating along with them. Part of the 2 + 2 = 5 synergy comes from the power of others working with you.

As Bertrand Russell said, "Some people would rather die than think, and some do." Stodgy managers find the soft creative process weird. They became addicted to their beliefs. In our culture, constant nose-to-the-grindstone determination remains a virtue, with examples ranging from John Paul Jones to Thomas Edison. But the many hours these heroes spent in incubative solitude do not make exciting copy for history books; so we don't hear about that aspect of their success. The advice of an old-timer I met on a wooden bridge applies here, and I hope the poker-faces at work grasp the concept eventually: "Make the big decisions with your heart, and the little ones with your mind." The heart, intuition, a well-enriched, relaxed subconscious—these are all the same. Emerson said, "All great discoveries come from people whose feelings run ahead of their thinking." Enough said.

Some recommend that those having trouble loosening up to the creative process wear different color hats, literally, for the type of thinking they need to be doing at the moment. When wearing the clown's suit, it's easier to play the clown; inhibitions leave. You may also need a ritual to turn your creative switch ON. I know a guy who can be creative only when he doesn't wear socks. He said he never fully recovered from the regimentation of a firm he worked for that had an enforced requirement to wear socks. Not doing so now tells his subconscious he's rebelling, and the creative juices flow. Some firms have "informal Friday" where the suits and ties stay home. This change often works because the creative juices flow better on Fridays; the mind-numbing tasks get ground out on other days. Many firms have made all days informal for even better results. Similarly, some teams escape to off-site, serene places for creative decision-making. I sit in the woods.

Some of us received too much guidance on being "predictable." It's okay, if not necessary, to turn the creativity switch on and off for the occasion. Plan two purely creative mornings a week—unspoiled by monotony, stress, or fear. Turn the answering machine on and leave the area. I have a special cubbyhole in my home, a park bench, and a rustic deck that I have never let become "contaminated" with paperwork, boredom, or phones. Some firms have libraries where visionaries hide.

Oftentimes, if you're nice to it, the subconscious awards you with crystal-clear, intuitive solutions, worked out with every detail. At other times the message often knocks lightly, probably in your stomach. For example, you decide to take a job in Atlanta, but it just doesn't "feel" right. Your intuition wants something else that will be better for you in the long term.

Try this. When you have a yes-or-no decision to make, planning to follow chance, flip a coin. If the outcome creates a queasy feeling, your subconscious is telling you to go the other way. Believe the subconscious; it has no ego or fear. Convert as many decisions as you can to yes-no choices, just so you can use the coin-flipping exercise.

Over the years, I kept a tally: my intuition versus the other decision. My gut feel has won about nine to one. (When my intuition proved wrong, inadequate enrichment lurked in the background.) A few times correctly following my intuition first seemed to levy a price. Wide-angled vision led me into a vaguer direction, filled with more issues and questions than answers. But I later found myself better off temporarily being generally correct (with a few minor, temporary problems) than forever precisely wrong. The mystics tell us that distress exists to elevate us to a higher level of thinking. As I once heard a mystic religious leader say, "You can't know good if you haven't known bad."

Your subconscious works overtime when you sleep since there's no contamination from ego and fear. Save big issues for dropping-off-to-sleep times. Introduce them to the subconscious and ask for answers; use visualization and then set the issue aside. Above all, trust that answers will come, because they will, sometimes in mysterious and wonderful ways.

———————————————

Tonight's assignment: Go to bed an hour early so you will wake naturally and can lie still for a few minutes to evaluate your dreams. Before falling asleep, tell your subconscious to provide balance to your life, to guide you. Do this exercise every night until you notice the message. My wife did it for a week several months ago. She had recurring dreams of eating exotic and different foods. She later learned the dreams' meaning. She had a severe vitamin deficiency that had to be addressed. Her subconscious, in touch with all her bodily functions, knew it and tried to satisfy the need while she slept.

Sleep deprivation, intoxication, and stress interrupt normal sleep patterns and dreams. When the subconscious cannot achieve balance, you may be headed for burnout or a breakdown. Scary? You bet! If you don't remember your last dream—almost every night—you aren't getting enough sleep to rid your body of the daytime stress toxins.

According to most mystics, dreaming provides a

balance, or escape, from our destructive worldly fragmentation: male-female, black-white, Democrat-Republican, liberal-conservative, Christian-Jew. Higher-level thinkers see everything interconnected. Our fragmentation may be in the karma to destroy the world; our balancing dreams may reflect our underlying need to maintain the species.

CHAPTER 4

Surrendering

Believing's half the battle. Learn how to trigger biochemical processes that become a catalyst for your creativity and new self.

You've learned ways to enrich the subconscious and how to begin to incubate, so now let's discover surrendering. This will lead to superordinary additional incubation.

One afternoon while I was writing the first draft of this book, everything stalled. The words on the paper read like the assembly instructions that come with a complicated child's toy, but I couldn't see the problem or the cause. Falling asleep that night, I gave the issue to my subconscious and asked for help. I made my conscious mind walk away from the problem. It worked. All night I dreamed of fascinating places and activities. My analysis of the dream: "Surrender; walk away from the manuscript for a few days; do different stuff to enhance incubation." So I obeyed. My wife and I took an all-day boat journey down the river to a wondrous waterside restaurant where the beautiful people go. The outing "whacked" my system back into creativity. The words flowed.

More profoundly, Linus Pauling—the only person receiving two unshared Nobel Prizes—reported introducing questions to his subconscious just before falling asleep, usually for two weeks. Then he surrendered. According to Pauling, his nurtured subconscious mind kept the question alive and put him at the right place and time for new information and thoughts to enter through his five senses. Sometimes the surrendering and incubating continued for years while he waited for knowledge gaps to be filled, to yield the final piece of a puzzle. His subconscious always became "enriched," and the answers came.

Create an "old sage" in your mind to whom you can toss your problems. Introduce issues to this wise person and trust that answers will come, because they will. Practice believing that your sage can protect you from your fears. When you learn to surrender to your sage, your subconscious will always incubate a game plan. The sage may be Jesus or whomever you like, real or imaginary. The most important part of the creative process comes from this trust—the surrendering. Trusting your sage relieves stress by aiding helpful biochemical processes. A mystic force also permeates, one words can't describe.

Surrender to your sage. Ask to be led to the correct experiences to achieve your goals through present-mindedness—not for material gifts.

Sometimes you get stymied, stuck up against a wall. If at first you don't succeed, surrender to your sage and walk away. ("Surrender" thus becomes an active verb.) You may have stressed yourself and closed your treasure chest from too close an attachment to the outcome.

When intense people get stymied and back away from a project, they often experience unnecessary stress.

(Someone—our VOJ— taught us never to give up.) The stress prevents further incubation, and the treasure chest stays locked.

Surrender. Give the problem to your sage. Go have some fun. Do "different stuff." Then work on a new project. Your subconscious will nudge you when it has an answer. So pay attention.

You may want a different sage for various phases of your life: work, family issues, spiritual matters. You may have specialized "guardian angels" if you have a complicated existence. Give them names and talk to them frequently. The mystics speak of helpers from the spiritual world, maybe from another dimension—beyond length, width, height, and time. These servants won't come until you learn to relax, to surrender, to shed the outer self, which is the subject of this book. All great artists, performers, industrialists, and leaders speak of receiving many miraculous "breaks" during their rise to greatness. It seems they may have had help. The mystics call their helpers "guardian angels"; undecided creative folks may say of such visionaries: "No, their unattached surrendering simply enabled them to keep the energizing biochemical processes churning."

Some mystics believe that a person's guardian angel exists in a parallel universe to his higher spiritual self, a state achieved only during presentmindedness and surrender. It doesn't matter how it happens; it is only important that you be aware of the magic and believe it happens. Once you start the transition, you'll "know" it happens.

The first and required step to intensify the assistance from your guardian angel is to believe such beings exist, which comes easy for the well-read enlightened. In recent research reports, quantum physicists boggle the mind with their discoveries about atomic matter and the origins of the universe. Their findings blast our doubtful A-B-C-1-2-3 perceptions of the world. For example, the bodies of the human race exist mostly as molecular space between vibrating electrons and protons. If compressed to pure matter (like black holes in outer space), a billion of us combined would fill only a small thimble. The entire earth would fit in a football stadium. In a way, scientists tell us, "We're not even here!" Our bounded understanding of the unknown—higher dimensions where spirits may dwell, parallel universes (which scientists say all exist)—remains about as limited as that of fish watching the rain. They see droplets hit the surface, but they don't have the foggiest idea about "the other side" from where the rain came—the clouds, the atmospheric conditions. But humans have options fish don't. We can explore through imagination and reading. The more you enrich your subconscious about the latest scientific findings, the easier it becomes to relinquish your overattachment to a higher power, to become more creative.

It's not only okay to back off and incubate for creative answers, it's usually necessary to surrender so you can lose attachment for a while. Schedule on your calendar those issues worthy of later thought. They'll wait. Forget them for now.

Try these more subtle approaches for global issues that don't seem to have discrete parts that can go onto your "get-back-to-you-later calendar." Imagine you've been carrying a heavy bag through a big airport for several hours; feel the physical stress and bodily aches. Envision this scene for at least sixty seconds. Now, imagine your problems as articles in the satchel. Set it down and relax in a comfortable chair. Address your sage and ask that the problems stay in the bag for a while.

Try another technique called "clearing a space for yourself." Imagine you moved into a new house five minutes ago. Boxes impose everywhere and leave no place to walk, but you need space to sit and work creatively. Picture each of your distracting problems as sealed in a box. Depict the movers beforehand packing and taping them, individually, at your old house. Concentrate on this scene for at least thirty seconds (about how long it takes for the body's biochemical processes to trigger). Now, knowing what's in each box, mentally stack them aside to make room in the floor. Relax and enjoy the space. The boxes will wait for you to "unpack" them.

Similarly, the moving-day exercise works well for sorting out the past, especially when a situation has gone "real bad." Don't let unpleasant experiences lay idle. After a day of incubation, find a quiet place and sort out the lessons learned. Then mentally pack them away in the "moving boxes" and advance to the next new experience. A mystic considers everything a learning encounter. Experience it; then leave it.

When anxiety for the future has you completely overwhelmed, try making a list of your worries. Put this slate away in an envelope, telling your subconscious, "I'll get back to these." Ask your sage to remind you of them later and to help you forget them for now. Then go to a different and invigorating place to wallow in your present-mindedness. Every time anxiety creeps in, clue your subconscious that all your worries wait in that envelope.

For a long-term "whack," date this envelope and don't re-open it for eighteen months. You'll see that the worries never materialized, or that your creative present-mindedness enabled you to eliminate them.

Rigid people scoff at these mental ploys, but rest assured that most of the stress you feel imposes only mentally—it's an inside job. The danger usually isn't really standing right there in front of you. Something's tricked your body into going out of control. The same "something" can prevent you from dealing with the anxiety.

I stumbled across this attachment "hang-up" many years ago during simple times of uncomplicated automobiles, when we shade-tree mechanics could fix them with an adjustable wrench and a screwdriver. My neighbor and I had similar old cars we had to work on about half our Saturday mornings. I found myself about ten times more innovative diagnostically and mechanically with his car than with my own. The same for him; he was better on mine. Why? I stayed unattached to the outcome for his car and could surrender, to let my knowledge incubate and slip over from my subconscious. I remained uptight about my own junker; I had to drive it to work Monday morning. I couldn't "play" with it. I didn't know then that unattached, spontaneous people have faith and act; others worry.

Similar situations abound. I know a stockbroker who makes oodles of money for his clients, but often loses his own. He stays too attached to his outcome and can't follow his own good advice.

A theme of most religions, "Be in the world, but not of the world," becomes clearer when you discover how overattachment poisons your incubation and kills your life-enriching creativity. Some devout sects take this principle to extremes. But with moderation, the idea certainly applies to the creative part of your life. Overattachment locks the treasure chest and keeps incubated answers from escaping.

———————————

The following pages apply to organizational barriers to

creativity. You can skip to the next chapter if you do not supervise anyone and are sure you never will. Or you may find this section useful when dealing with family and friends. Perhaps you unintentionally dampen their creativity, which in turn drains your enthusiasm. (If you "tick off" your spouse, he or she may see to it that you pay.)

Fear, the subject of one of Edwards Deming's famous fourteen points, massacres creativity every time—closing treasure chests. Stated another way: when someone simply takes the attitude of defending a mistake, that person has little hope of improvement. "People who become good at making excuses seldom become good at anything else," Ben Franklin did say. Their brains don't incubate creative solutions because of the guilt and energy spent "making it through the day." (You can become an idiot forever if you get promoted into a job you're not ready for and have to constantly make excuses to keep the boss off your back.) Better companies outlaw finger-pointing. They've learned that people need to be unafraid to fail.

Many managers do not realize that only higher purpose motivates sustained constructive change. Fear and getting something by the boss do not make a higher purpose. Such anxiety prowls about as low as it goes when it comes to purpose. That's especially true when your boss's agenda for you involves making him look good at the expense of bottom-line profitability. For creative folks, this purpose lurks so low, it ranks right down there with killing kittens. The mystics say that the motivation of an action—not the bigness or smallness of the action itself—affects an individual's personal consequences, or his karma. Knowing this truth, your subconscious causes you to become distressed by your contrived urgings, even though you may not be aware of the source of your gloom. (Committed, higher-level thinkers must experience a sense of peace founded in the rightness of the task.) If this description fits your situation and wrecks your creativity, find a new boss. (I am assuming that becoming more creative and enjoying a balanced life rank near the top of your priorities.)

A basic theme emerges repeatedly from research. A great workplace contains trust; it is one where no one requires you to "act" in any prescribed way, one where you do not fear back-stabbing. Going against intuition and "acting" in a business setting often leads to a creativity-draining quagmire—one in which employees do not control their own thoughts, not to mention their guilt. Innovative workers frequently will not remain and tolerate such "Gestapo tactics." Or they may remain and eventually lose their enthusiasm. "Housekeepers," who like to maintain the status quo, almost always stay. If you are in such an environment, make your choice either to get out or to live with it. Then cheer up.

About seventy-five percent of your associates fear speaking up, which is a sort of overattachment. Their motivation is less anxiety of being fired than fear of repercussion, especially of losing face. If the managers who need to heed this advice would follow my warning, this would be "the book to end all books." (But most of them don't read—or listen, or observe, or empathize, or think, or incubate, or empower, or improve, or compliment their spouses, or build forts with their kids out of blankets and chairs.)

Peter Drucker once said, "Most of what we do as managers prevents someone from doing their job." When it comes to innovation or often messy creativity, he's certainly correct. The classic bureaucratic model—still taught in many business courses—promotes sameness, limits choices, reduces options, and outlaws spontaneity.

And superficially, it works. Too well. Administrators often favor predictability over innovativeness, at all costs. Yet at times the chaos still breathes, festering below the surface in the hearts of the employees. They become working stiffs when their spirits wither, and often it is impossible to recover their enthusiasm. Intuitive, natural leaders never let this situation develop in the first place. They remain unblocked and maintain a reputation for open-mindedness. Friends and co-workers drench them with innovative, subconscious-enriching facts and ideas.

Creativity uncovers options, lots of alternatives. Innovation gets disordered at times, especially at first. Creativity questions all rules and involves free-wheeling—of the mind, and at times of the body too. Unenlightened supervisors often find it difficult not to impede this magic. That's why one theme of this book involves keeping most creative ideas to yourself until incubated and later "verified." At least, don't posit an immovable stance on issues that can be (dis)proven with data or facts. Natural leadership usually involves action, not position.

We all see gurgling, festering situations repeatedly: many brilliant employees who used to be creative, along with lots of missed opportunities, selfish personal agendas, and boss-watching. And generally the resumes go out, leading to whispered phone conversations with headhunters. When people can't feel good about their motivations, they feel miserable about their jobs and seldom produce creative ideas. The emphatic biochemical processes of the brain have shut down. (Their life expectancy may become fifteen years less.) (See REFERENCES, Fellers, *Why Things Go Wrong.*)

One example among many: when unreasonable budgets and incentive systems cause departments to plot against each other, commitment to the company gets cut in half.

Similarly, several independent studies report that when employees simply sell time for dollars (versus making a contribution to their life's goals), employers get about fifty percent out of them. Many of us have learned to look busy, and have internalized this skill to the point that we often welcome the warm feeling of being anesthetized by trivia. Adding to the bottom line all too frequently never becomes an issue, but drifting with the flow does.

"Absorb" this book. Then you'll develop detached boldness—the opposite of apathy. It's not as difficult as it sounds, but it does take practice. Read on.

Someone once told me that about forty percent of the population has wart virus for brains and will never embrace the creative (intuitive) approach. He may have been correct, but we can't know who has wart brains until they have an opportunity to show some enthusiasm—even if just for short creative periods. You can never effectively determine another person's commitment until you observe that individual in a job he likes, a job where he works because he wants to accomplish a worthwhile goal—not "doing in" other departments or colleagues because of bureaucratic overmanagement and boss-watching. Burned-out working stiffs develop a warped sense of obligation: when the boss is looking, "duty" consists of pretending the trivial to be important. Their spirit has died. It's impossible to be a natural leader in this situation. Enthusiasm can't be forced.

The old approach to business, involving back-stabbing and rugged individualism, doesn't work very well in today's environment, filled with complex problems requiring heightened creativity. That's why issues often get stuffed below the surface—beneath layers of bureaucracy, politics, boss-watching, and numbed minds—where incubation stalls.

If your organization reeks rotten with rules and procedures—if it suffers from corporate constipation—then you can't recommend this book to your boss's boss for fear. But you can still begin your own personal transition. Your newfound enthusiasm and creative improvements may get lots of attention. Find a long-term problem and incubate it privately, following this book exactly. Marvel others with your solution, before the issue becomes the "emergency of the day." Maybe you can muster up and maintain your excitement until in a position to slide this book onto your boss' desk.

Others will see your enthusiasm and what can be gained. Upper management changes only under two conditions: when there's no choice, or when there's something to be gained. Your personal benefit may be a shining example of what can be achieved. You can also use your new intuitive insight at home. All's not lost if your company's not ready for creative people constantly in a good mood from a natural creative "high" and from having time to embrace the creative process.

CHAPTER 5

Making Time

Gain a half-day a week with little up-front time investment. The uncluttered mind becomes less stressed, more efficient, more creative, and a fun place to spend the day.

Take a review break. Read items 1-6 in the appendix before proceeding. (Don't ignore this suggestion!)

Feeding the subconscious and allowing incubation takes time. All creative people squeeze in moments to "gaze out the window." They develop a reverence for time. They rarely let others cast frenzies upon them. Insight and guidance often come down as lightly as falling snow. (You can't run past it and expect to see it.) Time is nature's way of keeping all things from happening at once. Time-out for dreaming becomes a safe way to test options for the future. (Dreaming and absentmindedly gazing off into space differ. The advice from the mystics: pay attention.)

If you'll often seek additional time to engage in different and unique activities, you'll develop a "search image" for work-reducing ideas. Consider the following.

Make sure your subconscious knows your long-term

intentions, so you can appropriately prioritize. How do enthusiastic people draw on a source of inspiration seemingly unfathomable to working stiffs? Here's how: they've learned to associate their present work with their life's purpose. A connection usually exists if you look for it. Nothing becomes totally routine or boring if it supports your greater life's purpose.

The issue seldom involves a new job. (You've heard about the not-always-greener grass.) Careful contemplation can generally reveal why you stay in your current position and how it supports your personal goals. But there may be a necessary career diversion here and there—and for good reasons. The mysterious subconscious knows your final destination and will help direct you there. Some of my worst jobs and projects led me to my present level of thinking. It's mystical what led me into and out of them so I could gain the knowledge to move on to my true "calling." Establish your life's purpose and the same will happen to you. Try this: in the middle of a long vacation, go alone to the seashore or a mountainside. Spend the first two hours intensely observing nature, the next two mentally reliving your entire life, and the last two evaluating why you do what you do. The answers will come, especially if you first surrender to your sage asking for help.

The do-this-and-you'll-get-that behaviorist nature of our world will have you jumping around like a rat in a Skinner maze looking for a morsel of food. The subconscious knows this knee-jerking usually goes against human nature—which thrives on contemplation, questioning, and spirituality. Not coming to grips with "why am I doing this?" throws the subconscious into discord. The treasure chest closes.

You will become more creative one small step at a time at first; but when you make the *total* transition toward creativity, there will be a point where you begin to believe in magic. (Keep this fact to yourself.) Creativity becomes a mystical path. A creative person is a medium from a higher power, and others' doubt will dampen his trust, by reducing something transcendental to something mundane.

To a person in touch with his intuitive powers, everything fits together. As you become more intuitive, it will seem that no chance events occur (or have occurred) in your life. The mystics call this magic "synchronicity"—the fortunate intermeshing of events. Some quantum physicists take this principle a step further. They suspect that synchronicities come from more than a mystical mental programming or karma. They believe that through subtle psychokinesis (PK) human thought processes interconnect with the physical world in ways not yet fathomable to the normal mind. (In other words, we're like the fish watching the rain.) If you want a good "whack," read *Hyperspace* by admired physicist Michio Kaku. *The Holographic Universe* by Michael Talbot will "whack" you again. To these advanced scientific minds, anything seems possible. As soon as you introduce their mathematically proven concept of higher dimensions to your subconscious, anything will seem conceivable: ghosts, UFOs, near-death experiences, a heaven, or even shamanism—the belief that some trained individuals can access ancestral spirits from another dimension.

Knowing your life's purpose and having "seen the future," your subconscious will see to it that you gain all the correct enrichment—by being at the right places at the right times. Whether this phenomenon is mystical, or explained by quantum physics (or both), who knows? But when you reach this state, you'll tap into the "energy" that mystics discuss. (And you'll have no problem transferring this spirit to people around you.) When you arrive at this point, only possible when you know your *true* life's purpose, the advice offered by the mystics applies: "Visualize and wish for it, and it will come true." Then synchronicities will occur. So be careful what you ask.

Tibetan mystics speak often of karma, a sort of a preprogrammed cause and effect. Your karma comes partly from your "reason for existing," and works largely through your subconscious and visualization. My karma included writing this book. Your karma included reading it.

This mysticism and your wishes contain a hitch: if you've "tapped the energy," you won't ask for ego-centered possessions or experiences not supportive of your life's purpose. Sounds mystical? It is.

At the surface, many seemingly have disproved the advice of spiritual leaders: "Ask, and you shall receive." Out of context this advice isn't true; in context it is. This advice only applies to some people: those who have cast off their old life (the outer self) and also gotten in touch with their life's purpose. These folks do not ask for ego-centered materialistic things. They only ask to be guided through the correct experiences to fulfill their calling. The subconscious takes over from there.

One exception pertaining to wishes: when it's your time to die, you die; your job's done. All mystics agree on this point. But the mystics also explain that the body often flirts with death so that the spiritual person will respond through prayer or meditation, and present a positive example for someone not in touch with his inner self. Or as other mystics teach: it takes pain to raise an individual to the next higher level of thinking. Another exception: life threats can reveal your *true* life purpose. Then you pull through to accomplish "why you're here."

Once you've "tapped the magic," you'll also become

increasingly unattached, and thus more creative. You'll notice a curious transformation: you'll possess a feeling that you will survive no matter what happens. You won't even fear death—a time when you grasp a "heavenly" knowledge undreamed of on earth. As Mohammed said, "Life is a dream; when we die, we wake." For the living, the dying he spoke of refers to losing the ego. Being alive— and thus asleep—has become a nightmare for some. They experience hell on earth, anguish from overattachment and a failure to surrender—not establishing present-mindedness to discover and learn another approach.

Knowledge and learning appear in the teachings of most mystics. Many believe that "we're here" mostly to gain knowledge. Advanced creativity exists in the cosmos, and is available only to those experiencing the magic of surrender and unattachment. (It's all a game; the choices make it interesting.)

Negative thoughts of any sort crash this state of mind. That's why a large part of this book involves learning how to avoid (or to prevent) spiritually draining situations.

When you make the transition, you'll have peace whether or not you are outwardly successful. (However, the comfort of mind will enhance your chances of making creative decisions and choices that aid outward success.) Transformed innovators become less flattered by flattery, less blamed by blame, and take on a new sense of time— seldom being rushed, yet getting more accomplished through presentmindedness. Not driven by the ego, they also see things for what they are.

Set aside that six hours to reflect on your life's purpose, now. Some parts of this book may seem weird until you do this exercise and program your subconscious in the right direction.

Write a life's purpose and prioritize around what's really important—not the ego or Madison Avenue.

Changes in the world will be difficult to accept unless you have a changeless, internal sense of why you're here. This identity almost *never* comes from what others expect of you. Evaluate the sources of your struggles, your goals, your attitude toward material possessions, and what you want others to think about you. If professors, parents, ego-striving, or peer pressure come to mind in any way during this search, you've not likely found why you do what you do. Don't panic; just try again.

Another warning: if you've drenched yourself with expensive toys—from a BMW to a better home than you need—evaluate your motivations. These perks of success may be consolation prizes to make up for not doing what you truly want to do for a living. Instead, why not stockpile that hefty income? You may be able to eventually buy your way into your chosen career; or the nest egg may weaken an overattachment you have to your present job, making it more satisfying.

When employees determine their life's purpose, they usually become more productive in their present jobs. But when they find they must change vocations, everyone wins. No firm needs fifty-percent committed folks "selling time for dollars."

Success comes not from looking for it, but from being passionate about one's work and motives. We frequently see people working hard, but also boss-watching and maneuvering politically on the side, all the while subconsciously hating the sucking-up and fear of losing face over trivial issues. Distress closes their treasure chests. Many of these people only want to do rewarding work, to be secure, to make a contribution, and to become self-actualized through their efforts and results. Along the way somewhere they got misdirected—not in what they wanted to do, but in why they wanted to do it. Coming to grips with this issue will make their work more meaningful, and they will become more effective and creative. They can then manage their time by prioritizing around what's *really* important to them. They stop fearing they will fail to achieve something they never wanted in the first place.

Even in cases where people's upward career mobility exists in their karma (things meant to be), overattachment still often prevents them from achieving their ultimate status. Anxiety (loss of presentmindedness) about always having to "look good" prevents them from creatively "attending to the work at hand." They fail to realize that the path *is* the goal.

For some reason, the enhancing biochemical processes don't trigger unless fun comes from at least part of an activity. That's why a life's purpose sits atop of your most important mountain. Be a success at what comes enjoyable and almost effortless, or die struggling for something someone else (or no one else) wants for you. It's just that simple. Any mystic will tell you, "A lower mind cannot comprehend higher truths." Trying to discover your creative existence without understanding your life's purpose is like trying to hear the music by reading the notes off a sheet. (Of course, we all have the option of living the "lower" life.)

Many therapists recommend writing your own epitaph—what you want on your tombstone. Even better, write what you'd like folks to say about you at your funeral. Be especially concerned if the comments you want resemble these: "He was right after all," or, "Finally she rests." Such comments suggest a draining lifetime struggle. They also indicate that something is blocking the incubative processes of the subconscious. Don't be a "martyr." It just isn't worth it, not if you want to be creative and happy. If it's in your karma to change the world, and if you visualize based on your life's purpose, you will do this with little struggle. Life wasn't meant to be a struggle.

Try writing your real job description for both work and home. "Real" would be the way you'd explain it to a ten-year-old child, or the way she'd explain it to her friends. State two to three clear objectives, not what's in some old dusty manual. Try to avoid words or expressions like: "aids in, impacts, coordinates," or "interfaces with." Be more specific and you may be able to prioritize your work more effectively.

Your next project: design your perfect workday for five years out. Don't mention status, money, or position—only what you'd like to be doing from minute to minute. Visualize this perfect day for at least sixty seconds; focus on how it would feel—every detail. Tell your subconscious, "This will happen." Ask your sage for help. Meditate on the feeling again for thirty seconds. Within several months your subconscious will discover what's in your way of feeling this way at all times. Your subconscious will work on it and help you find time to do what it takes to get there. Now it knows the difference between how you want to feel and how you do feel. The subconscious hates dissonance. Listen to its nudges.

Visualization aids most everything you do. It helps your subconscious guide you into and through many nurturing circumstances, even when you're not aware of it. (For most circumstances, thinking something usually makes it so, even for bad stuff.)

You may not succeed at first, but keep trying. Nature

has a way of making sure you get visualization right, or don't get it at all. And luckily so. If your wishes "will happen," they had better be what you *really* want. If your subconscious doesn't know your life's purpose, or if ego forced the wrong one into your head, visualization remains next to impossible. Assuming you know why you do what you do, try the following ways to enhance visualization:

Listen to soothing music—which releases valium-type compounds in the body.

Wait until after sex.

Go sailing.

Go to the seashore, forest, or your childhood tree house.

Wait until just after a religious ceremony.

Try deep, slow breathing to get body and mind in sync.

Insure there's been a recent and pleasant sensation of all your senses. Bringing all five into play magically impresses the subconscious.

To enhance presentmindedness over the weekend, every Friday afternoon create a prioritized weekly list of work projects based on gut feeling—what you want to do most. Put this list aside and go into the weekend not worried about what you're "not worrying about." Come back on Monday raring to tackle what's most important. We usually self-initiate high-payoff endeavors, but in the daily frenzy we often fail to schedule time for them, especially when we ignore (or stymie) our intuition.

Another good exercise: decide what you would do career-wise if you won the lottery. Your subconscious probably tugs you in that direction. You can give in now or develop a hardened attitude by turning the other way. Or perhaps your career now, crummy as it may be, provides the money and security you need for a greater life's purpose outside work. You may need to accept the situation at the office and at home and cheer up. In the emerging "new age," people will avoid sourpusses who block others' creative juices.

Several times a day stop working, look at your priorities, and associate the day's activities with your life's purpose; in essence, be aware of yourself. You can only manage time when alert to what's going on within and around you. But don't panic during bad times. Some days, your creative juices aren't stirring. If you don't take this natural rhythm in stride, a bad day can have more go wrong in five minutes than an innovative one can in ten hours.

Divide and conquer, a concept missed by most procrastinators. Behavioral scientists use a phrase called "compulsion to closure." Finishing projects produces a warm feeling, biochemical nurturing and enthusiasm our subconscious thrives on. When you divide a big project into smaller, short-term pieces, completing each part relieves stress and opens the treasure chest. That is especially true if you prioritize the components and work on one issue at a time. A surefire stress reducer: attending to the work at hand, just getting lost in it, with no fear of what you *aren't* doing.

Set aside designated "crap days"—four-hour blocks during low-energy times to deal with paperwork and trivia. Get them on your calendar: then stop worrying about what you're *not* doing, and move on with creative thoughts.

———————————————

For time management, the wastebasket becomes your

best friend. We retrieve only five percent of what gets filed, so throw most papers away and don't waste time finding a place for them. You need a *definite* reason to keep correspondence. For me, if in doubt, file thirteen, here it comes! And you know, I can't remember the last time I couldn't find something. To keep your stress level down, establish a temporary trash can, or a desk drawer, and if there's any doubt about a piece of paperwork, chunk it in there. When full, discard the bottom seventy-five percent. You'll find no overly neat creative folks, but they generally have a level of organization beyond the normal person (for things important to them), thus lower stress and open treasure chests.

Some people suffer frazzled days: treasure chest often closed, frequently from trivial irritations. For example, they may constantly underestimate how long it will take to complete projects. They generally stay behind, not with someone else's schedule, but with their own self-imposed one. This becomes a particularly guilt-inducing, energy-draining situation. Stress ruins a lot of good days and closes many treasure chests. Here's a new approach: consider that everything will take twenty percent longer than estimated. (Actually, there's some industrial engineering theory behind this practice.) For me, it's working. From the calm within me, creative ideas now surface more often. My subconscious incubates. I get more accomplished. In the past, on bad days, I expected to be creative without providing time for contemplation. That's like telling one flower to grow and watering another.

So much for general principles. Now here's a laundry list of some specific time-management practices. Not a lot of deep psychology here, just useful tidbits. No single suggestion will matter a great deal. Do all of them and you may gain a half-day per week—about what you need for quiet, meditative, gazing-out-the-window moments: the fuel for incubation.

1. Don't review the obvious at meetings: production figures everybody knows, boring minutes from the last meeting.
2. Return calls before nine, just before lunch, after three, or at quitting time when people occupy their offices. The average person spends two years of his life on the phone. (That's more than most people take for vacations.)
3. Meet people in their offices. That way, you can leave at will.
4. Get an answering machine for home and work. Pay for it yourself if necessary.
5. Purchase a mobile phone and use call forwarding. It's difficult to maintain presentmindedness and to be creative with a dozen conversations in limbo.
6. Get a miniature, voice-activated recorder for your car and other time-wasting places. Make notes during long stretches on interstate highways. Record all hunches and spurts of insight—a large part of the creative process.
7. Treat bill paying and such like a business. Organize an office at home. You don't want to pitch your tent and dig your trenches every time you need to make camp.
8. If you're forgetful, use car and home hide-a-keys.
9. Have a re-organization Saturday. Go to work and do nothing but clean files, organize materials, and throw away junk. When I first started this "housecleaning," I gained two hours a week.
10. Handle mail only once standing over the wastebasket.

11. Put a discard date on everything filed so you and others can throw away outdated material (a good stress reducer).

12. Get an extra table top in your office. You won't need to put in-progress projects away when you move to something else. Like a child (and I say this positively), creative people often jump from one topic to the next. The also-productive creative folks arrange their work environment to make this activity possible.

13. Always highlight when reading. Your third-grade teacher's not around to yell at you for marking in books.

14. When interrupted, jot down what you were doing. It's easier to return.

15. During uncluttered hours, make lists of projects. For example, in airports with your calendar out. Go into the greatest detail: meeting take-with-you lists, attendance rosters, National Secretary Week dates, birthdays, and so forth. Organize by the week, based on what's important to you. (And don't let your life's purpose get too far away from the front of your mind.) Designate several items you *must* accomplish by week's end. Prioritize by the day, usually the evening before, so you can leave the stress at work. Put asterisks by required daily items. (I'm not just talking about trivial office work. I also break creative projects down into pieces and put them on a list.)

    You could get through most days without a roster, but for many borderline workaholics, the list lets them know when the day's over. If the asterisked items get done, they can go home without worrying about the unknown projects waiting to pounce on them the next morning.

By all means, allow looking-out-the-window time. (Pick unattached bold moments to make to-do lists. Then during later more doubtful periods *just do them,* not worrying about the reasons why not. Here's something a sage advised that changed my life: write ten things you'd do if you had unlimited courage; after several days of incubating, do at least five of them.)

16. Keep a carry-around-with-you file to be shuffled through at the dentist, while commuting, on airplanes. About ten percent of my not-quite-junk mail goes in there.

17. Stand when long-winded people enter.

18. Make a game out of little time-management gimmicks. An example: tear the corner off magazines so you'll never waste time looking through them again.

19. Get a small file cabinet you can reach from your chair. Most papers you need, you need often.

20. Learn how to file correctly. I need some lessons myself on this subject. My MISC file has *everything* in it.

21. Be a smart traveler. Packing for trips can cause stress. Two ideas: If you travel a lot, never unpack (except dirty clothes, of course). For long trips, start loading your briefcase several days in advance; you'll never arrive without articles, and won't get last-minute panic.

22. Plan ahead. When someone calls to set up a meeting, at that moment, get *all* the facts: the who, when, where, and what. Ask what to wear, what to bring, who's going to be there, how do you need to prepare, etc. It all goes on the calendar—right then. Within two minutes mark the days when you need to get ready. Schedule lots of incubation time and loads of opportunities to get your subconscious enriched. Then forget about it.

23. Prepare for each new day. Lay out your clothes and business materials the night before. Let's face it; you gotta get your stuff out anyway. Why not the night before? Peaceful mornings get you into a more creative mood for the day.

24. Accept the rhythm of life. Some times just aren't made to be creative. (Only the mediocre person is always at his best.) You'll learn to feel how the day is going to go by 7:00 A.M. What a chance to work like a dog and get lots of nagging and boring paper work out of the way to unclutter future high-energy days! "Surrender" to the bureaucracy on "down" days and don't feel guilty. Not following your bio-rhythms will contribute to burn-out.

25. Eat lunch at 1:00 P.M. when there's no rush. The noon hour provides great working time—no one calls.

26. Stay out of banks on Fridays. Some people still cash that check, feel the money, and go pay bills in person.

27. Try to use flex hours to avoid rush hour.

28. Take advantage of innovative ways to spend five minutes:

   a. Make an appointment.

   b. Make meeting attendance lists.

   c. Dictate a short letter on your recorder.

   d. Organize a file.

   e. Proof something.

   f. Order game tickets.

   g. Study and annotate your calendar.

   h. Work through your carry-around-with-you file.

   i. Call your spouse or kids for an emotional "fix."

**Make a game of saving time. Your most valuable
resource deserves constant attention.**

Someone once asked Napoleon why he was able to
defeat the mighty Austrians, and he said, "They never
learned how to use five minutes."

So now you know about the mysterious subconscious
and how to prime it for that all-important incubation—
plus ways to make some time for this process to happen.
Keep the mysticism to yourself. Crusty old naysayers will
laugh at you for being so philosophical. Your subconscious may hear them, or your own conscious mind may
send a misleading message into the treasure chest. Your
subconscious—delicate and a bit gullible—will often take
communications at face value. As you've probably heard,
you can't win an argument with an ignorant person.

Healers through the ages have had a deep understanding of the power of suggestion on the subconscious. They
have also understood how others can send doubt to
destroy the magic. Jesus healed two blind men, saying to
them, "According to your *faith* be it unto you." And note
what He said further to the once-blind men about telling
potential doubters, "See that no man know it." He knew
doubt could cause the two men to go back to blindness.
For some reason the Creator programmed many choices
into the karma for the universe.

The subconscious has a powerful—but delicate—effect
on the human mind and body. The forces of evil can
quickly regain control: the eternal and mystical challenge.

CHAPTER 6

Enhancing the Magic

The innovation-packed subconscious contains a treasure chest of knowledge, trying to escape. Learn how to defeat the creativity gate guards—to become unattached from time to time. Understand and put to practical use what the mystics have been telling us for several millennia.

You know about "whacking" the subconscious with varied facts and experiences. You've learned how to gain extra time to enable the subconscious to incubate—the magical 2 + 2 = 5 formula. Now let's look at ways to increase the odds that you can open your treasure chest when needed.

Usually the flow from the subconscious carries flashes of insight. They may be faint; they may be mind-boggling. Often they occur at dawn, in the car, or while in the shower. The message may be clear; it may be subtle and in the gut—especially for yes-no issues. Always be ready to set the hook. Pens, pencils, note pads, and recorders make up the tools of the creative person. Keep a supply handy on your night stand and near the shower. How many times have you forgotten a brilliant idea? You don't need this stress, and the world needs your inspiration. Record even hunches and insights. The subconscious often works in mysterious ways. When an idea pops up, never analyze it at the moment, just write it down. (Within twenty-four hours try to review your notes.)

Give intuitive flashes wide spaces in the shadows of your mind. Ignore for now analytical or stressful questions like: "How much will this cost?" "What will others think?" "How will this advance my career?" Many extraordinarily creative people have told me that setting the hook and not jumping to idea-killing conclusions or worrying about thought-stopping obstacles may be the biggest difference between them and less innovative people. They have also frequently expanded on how they had to practice to accomplish this feat.

To experience the flash of insight, lots of subtle activities come into play. Surrendering (not thinking about it) presents the biggest challenge. Pulling the plug with non-thinking (by playing an instrument, surrendering to your sage, exercising, fishing, going skiing, or taking a walk) will enhance creativity. But these work only if you're doing them purely for fun, not from ulterior motives, and not because you're stressed by competition.

I rarely smoke, but occasionally I go into the woods and have a cigar to cure writer's block. It works every time. I just give in. The taste, smell, and feel of the cigar and the preoccupation of trying to light it in the breeze (the non-thinking involved in the whole process) opens the treasure chest. This space between thoughts encourages the tricklings from the subconscious.

Both the secret of creativity and the thrust of this book involve learning to bring the spirit of childhood back into adulthood. Getting "lost" in an alert mental state stimulates this presentmindedness—the uncluttered Zen of no past and no future, just the present, the time when the wisdom of the subconscious seeps out. A sage said living with a child is like living with a sage. A child sees all things as they are. (If only children had the nuts-and-bolts skills to put their insights to practical use!)

When at work, stand up and stretch about every thirty minutes and always sit erectly. Keeping the blood circulating stimulates the brain. Place the coffee pot and pencil sharpener in another room. The frequent short walks provide a subtle "whack" and can calm you to give priority to your thoughts, as will exercise of any type.

Try this mental exercise for specific apprehensions or worries. Designate an article of clothing or jewelry as your source of potential anxiety, a "tension token" you can take off and hide. (This is a trick, but your mind plays games with you in the first place.) When you get that sinking-in-the-stomach feeling, ceremoniously cast away that symbolic piece of clothing—the tension token—and the stress with it. Practice frequently with small issues first, not the oncoming train.

I also use this tension-token idea when I need to elicit creative ideas from groups of hostile, disgruntled employees. Before we begin meetings, I ask them to write their gripes on index cards, in detail. I say, "We'll deal with these valid complaints in separate meetings. For now, let's keep the cards tucked away." I want them to understand that anger and anxiety kill creativity, and to be willing to set them aside temporarily.

Pay attention to your dreams. The borderland between sleep and waking presents a magical time, holding its own rhythm not to be ignored. Lie in bed and review every dream at length. Associate each detail with your problems and opportunities. Look for recurring patterns. Dreams reveal uninhibited seepage from the subconscious, and they always symbolize something, especially repeating dreams. The body and mind seek balance, and the subconscious often tries to provide the equilibrium during dreams, when treasure-chest closers don't exist. Getting enough sleep and having a few minutes to lie in bed and rethink your last dream will pay big for you. Just before and after deep sleep, the brain transitions from its potentially uptight beta state to the slowed-down alpha state—the time proved best for imprinting thoughts onto the subconscious.

If you do not wake naturally in the morning, you do not get enough sleep. Your dream patterns get interrupted, and the result may be eventual mental instability or burnout. (It has been estimated that forty percent of the population doesn't get enough sleep.) Publicized geniuses reportedly sleep short nights. But they can take creativity-enhancing catnaps anytime during the day to remove stress toxins—like the dog or cat who can howl at 3:00 A.M. if he prefers. We eight-to-fivers can't do that; so forget what you've read about folks doing well on just a few hours sleep. That's probably not for you if you want to be a creative clear-thinking person. The normal person needs to snooze long enough to transition into the deep-sleep state of delta and theta brain waves, both associated with creative imagery and deep thought.

Creativity comes when the person is totally in the present; it's the only way. Every time my mind wanders into the future—my next project, activities others want me to be doing, what my copyeditor will do to my latest manuscript, or when I'm going to get around to paying the bills—my creativity collapses. I stop working, list all my anxieties, and put notes on my calendar to think about these things later. The presentmindedness returns and enables me to float above it all. I can get lost in the work before me, at least for a while.

> **Become a fanatic about presentmindedness: attending to the work at hand. Make appointments on your calendar to think about distractions later.**

When getting involved with a client's problems, I do not monopolize the discussion. I sit and listen with no personal agenda. Talking can in itself close the treasure chest. (That's why it's recommended you keep your newfound source of enthusiasm to yourself for several months. Don't destroy the peace by speaking needlessly.) Why do infants absorb so much? They have no choice but to listen. Hearing and listening become different activities when you become your new creative self.

In your silence you'll learn to laugh at your old self. A mystic once said, "Angels can fly because they take themselves so lightly."

Humor and creativity go hand in hand. The most obvious reason: laughter leads to stress reduction which improves presentmindedness as a result of better blood flow to the brain and the releasing of energizing endorphins. Humor also takes you back to your childhood, when happenings weren't so serious, and you sometimes forgot to be uptight. But something else equally powerful also happens with laughter.

The human brain always tries to sort thoughts into place, at all costs, to make the connection and move hastily to the next issue. It quickly tries to set up a pattern, whether or not the components relate.

Humor forces incompatible or contradictory situations into the mind at the same time. (As an example: sex is nobody's business except the three people involved.) This forces the brain to make a connection—as it does when the mind is creating. When in a problem-solving mode, this mixing of unlikeness often yields the creative $2 + 2 = 5$ synergy (or at times $2 + 2 = 1,000$). Laughter provides good practice in connecting dissimilar ideas and warms up the creative might.

So now you see; all my jokes and snide remarks throughout this book had a larger purpose. I wanted to get you out of the predictable. Pleasant "shock" opens treasure chests. Stuffiness can keep them closed—as will nagging spouses, bosses looking at you with a frown over the top of their reading glasses, and traffic cops shaking their finger at you.

Creative people see connections and patterns others don't and learn to relate seemingly dissimilar concepts. Humor provides their practice field, especially when they laugh about the specific issue or problem at hand. Make it funny, and the subconscious may reward you. (Of course, laugh under your breath, or in the parking lot.) The humor may dredge up from the subconscious a connection undreamed of until now. (I've known many caring, useful people with no sense of humor, but never a creative one.)

Along similar lines, try thinking opposites to "whack" the brain out of its lazy patterns. Experiment with defending a foe's position—just for fun. Also, think negatives: "What will the customer hate about this design?" "If Sam gets promoted, what will everyone else think?" "How do the employee-of-the-month awards affect the losers; could their loss in morale cost more than the worth of the winners' fleeting adrenaline flush?" When I get involved with a business client in a do-or-die, turn-around undertaking, I often purposely think the *opposite* of the local executives. They look at today and try to guess what's wrong. I do the opposite and pretend we're already successful and profitable. After "enriching" my subconscious with the facts and incubating for several days, I visualize (for at least sixty seconds) their success and let my subconscious "feel" the disharmony. Then I ask myself: "What in the present situation would prevent them from staying prosperous?" The reason they got into a mess usually becomes clear.

Imagine how someone else would solve the problem: a banker, Winston Churchill, a ten-year-old, your spouse, Forrest Gump. I always ask myself what Bob Newhart would do. Or my grandparents. Growing up before Sputnik, the welfare state, twenty-two-year-old fast-talking MBAs, a useless war, and two-million-dollar lawsuits for coffee too hot at McDonald's, our elders often have a down-home creative nature—especially after they retire and no longer have job anxieties.

Another suggestion: before you access your sage, keep a problem constantly in your mind. Not in a stressful or anxious way, but enough to impress on your subconscious the importance of working this one through and, of course, in time for you to gather the facts you need to reach a decision. (That's the enrichment.) I trust my subconscious to hold the information for me, but I still generally write down what information I've gathered. This may help reduce the worry that I might forget something. Or maybe it helps my subconscious realize: "Here's some important stuff!"

Toss the issue around, play with it; but be patient and do not expect, or even allow, a final answer to flow too quickly. I put decision dates on my calendar. This act gives me permission to remain playful during the interim. Look for reasons to succeed, not excuses why alternatives will fail. If you think you have a solution, write it down to get it off your mind, and go back to tossing ideas around, maybe for several days. Redefine the problem in every way you can. Above all, suspend judgment and let the subconscious incubate. When you turn a problem over to your sage, be patient. The big picture will come; the details will follow.

The wisdom from the subconscious often flows delicately, like whispers, faint and far away. Everyday life can close the subconscious down tight, often to rust shut. Surrendering, reducing attachment, and suspending judgment become the crowbars that re-open it, with practice, even if just for an hour here and there. Presentmindedness can help you solve or eliminate the root causes of the stress that closed you down tight in the first place. That's what happened to me. Life's funny; its problems can keep us from solving its problems. Bad gets worse, or better becomes best.

CHAPTER 7

Letting Go

Some fear and stress remain unavoidable, but you can learn to reverse their effect during creative times. Discover how to make temporary "space for yourself."

If you're over the edge with stress, see your doctor. I'm not an M.D. and can't help you if your electrolytes flow so badly out of balance your eyes don't focus, you twitch about the face and neck, or your lips move uncontrollably. If something profound has left you depressed or suicidal, also see a doctor.

But I do know how to deal with self-imposed superficial stress. So let's begin. Watch yourself become more intuitive as you learn to relax. You'll even get smarter when you learn to "set anxiety aside."

Stress produces a dangerous chemical wash of cortisols—which actually kill off nerve cells in the brain while trying to regulate stress. Anxiety also floods the gray matter with unused adrenaline, causing blood to rush from the extremities. The blood also becomes thicker so it can coagulate quicker, in case a tiger encroaches the cave to bite and claw.

If irritants in your environment set you off, get them behind you first. Generate a running list over several days of controllable, trivial nuisances. Eliminate them all, like a bulldozer moving dirt. Minor stresses, along with big problems, multiply together to yield unwanted synergy. Eliminating trivial irritants can collectively pay big.

Typical trifling (but ruinous) stressors include:

Family demands—like the kids meeting you at the door after work with their requests. Impose a fifteen-minute grace period during which you can browse the mail, shuffle the newspaper, sit on the deck, or do whatever you choose. (Allow kisses and hugs only.)

Noise, at work and at home. Purchase some good earplugs for yourself and buy the kids some thirty-dollar stereo earphones. Run the dishwasher, vacuum, and other disgusting noise-makers other than at prime times.

Odors (or for that matter, anything sensory). Unpleasant aromas can hinder creativity. Wholesome smells do the opposite. For example, Alan Hursch, M.D., director of the Smell and Taste Treatment and Research Foundation in Chicago, proved that the scent of green apples increases the brain's alpha waves—a phenomenon associated with alert relaxation and incubation in the subconscious. The aromas of oranges, basil, clove, and lavender also induce relaxation. Similarly, have you noticed your change of mood when you enter someone's home during the holidays and smell potpourri-laced cider steaming on the stove? A soothing biochemical process begins.

Missing objects. Get an extra TV remote control, just for you, and attach it to your chair with Velcro. Keep extra light bulbs, razors, tissue, and such on hand. Buy zillions of extras for things you can never find. For me it's jogging socks, reading glasses, and super glue. Have so many, they find you.

Dirty house and car. A clean home and vehicle brighten your day. Run all your cars through the car wash every week putting to-do items on your calendar while you wait. Divide the home chores, in writing if necessary, and do them on a regular basis.

Disorganization and rush. Work mornings make a particularly stressful time. Lay everything out the evening before. Buy a coffee maker with a timer. Move the vehicle that leaves first to the driveway exit the night before. Keep car keys in the same place—always. Even plan breakfast and set the table the night before.

The telephone. Get an extra phone line for the kids. Refuse to talk to telemarketers.

Unnecessary chatter. Make it a rule: no talking before the first morning coffee. Stop the car and hand the keys to nagging backseat drivers. Tampered-with brains become mush, and never create.

The month you spend ridding your environment of

little irritants will be some of the best work of your life. Don't put up with irritations: destroy them—and enjoy it! The most miserable and uncreative people I know tolerate and suffer.

Stress can accumulate slowly, making it impossible to see the month-to-month build-up. Get with your spouse, coworker, or closest friend and mull over this list of early, sneaky stress indicators:

Getting sick more often.

Exploding more easily.

Changed desire for food, sex, or socialization.

Increased drug or alcohol use.

Sleeping poorly.

More frequent headaches.

Worsening digestive discomfort.

Becoming more forgetful—especially of names.

Losing your train of thought.

Spending less time on hobbies you love.

Beginning to look like your driver's license picture.

Crying over movies that "aren't really that sad."

Beginning to lose confidence in yourself.

Generally feeling further behind at 5:00 P.M.

Increasing indecisiveness, teeth gritting, frowning, hair loss, plus jaw and neck pains.

Rapid weight gain or loss.

Poor grooming and dress, tardiness, increased finger and foot-tapping, minor accidents, making more excuses.

Increase in sighs or breathing releases.

Cold hands against your face, or feet against a partner—a telltale sign. (The fight-or-flight response steals warming blood from the extremities.)

Psychiatrists say that most, if not all, non-chemically based mental discord comes from overattachment: to a person, to assets, to a perception of how someone else should act, to an image. Most of our stress—founded or not—relates to overattachment to false notions about ourselves. We mistakenly think we must be popular, we must be important, we must be wise. The mystics say that we need only strive to be decent and happy human beings to initiate productive creativity.

You begin the transition from stress of overattachment to creativity with the guidelines of this book—present-mindedness, subconscious enrichment, incubation, aligning with your life's purpose, and so forth. Everything will begin to fall into place through mysterious synchronicities. If wealth and fame occupy your karma (the only time they will occur anyway), you're more likely to achieve them happily when you unpretentiously seek this higher level of thinking. Otherwise, you'll burn out.

You may think you'll never reach your "higher self" as long as the low-life lurks in the next office (or on the other side of your bed), but you can. Temporarily "creating space for yourself" will direct you to a way to deal with those keeping your treasure chest closed—generally a way leaving no dead losers bleeding on the battlefield.

———————————

If you think you become more productive—not to mention creative—by pushing far beyond your limits week after week, you're dead wrong. Choose your lifestyle, not your deathstyle. Between sixty and ninety percent of illness comes from stress shutting down the immune system. It tells the body, "Why bother?" And sick people can be neither productive nor creative. Who has among the lowest life expectancy? People with lots of stress: dentists, cops, waiters and bartenders who have to put up with a lot of distress, executives, and people (in general) held responsible for occurrences they can't control. Many mystics have an interesting definition of hell: caring the most when the least powerful.

Listen to and read about centenarians: They all dodged stress. They didn't learn to cope; they avoided stress.

Fatigue comes as a part of life, and at times I still savor the feeling of having worked myself to exhaustion—a single day here and there. But this overexertion shuts my creative juices down for about a week. I accept this situation and don't push myself beyond my limits. I schedule "different stuff" to break the vicious pattern and to avoid burnout.

If you want to be innovative, remember: creativity comes after the calm, during those times when the mind unwinds and the treasure chest opens, when wisdom seeps from the subconscious, when the body, mind, and soul remain detached. Part of working hard smartly involves creative unwinding.

You certainly need to care about outcomes, but if you let overattachment stress you, the treasure chest closes. A good question to ask yourself is: "Will it matter five years from now?" If not, it ain't gonna kill ya! And it may need to be further down your list of priorities. Here's an even better question: "Am I doing this just to impress someone, or to uphold a false image?" We often let the trivial (or the ego) sap energy from our most important issues. Once you're burned out from pushing yourself beyond your limits, relighting the candle in the strong wind of despair will take time.

A few more physical suggestions: when wear from a normal day drains your energy, down a giant glass of water (or two), especially if you're a coffee drinker. This sudden influx activates your lymphatic system and revitalizes you. You won't believe how well it works for the two o'clock slump. Also, take multiple vitamins with lots of B-complex and calcium. The brain uses calcium for some of its relaxation chemistry. Stress depletes the store of B-vitamins. Researchers in Holland also showed that 20 milligrams of B6 every day for twelve weeks improved long-term memory. (My doctor won't say diddly to me about vitamins, but he takes them.) If I go several days without B-vitamins, I can feel the heightened impact of stress.

Rigorous exercise reduces stress by producing calming endorphins, as does singing or sitting in whirling water.

Don't skip a meal. Your body needs three to five small feedings a day, as does your stress-handling systems. (As an aside: most slim folks nibble frequently.)

If unavoidable spirit-drainers prowl in your life, buy a sand-filled punching bag. I persevered through a rigorous graduate program by imagining a sandbag as a certain unrealistic professor's revolting, twitching face. Later, I did the same for an idiot boss. Bag punching, tree kicking, and such physical activities positively trick the brain, but most stress comes from the brain's habit of fooling you. Learning to live with something—in a civilized way—often just pushes the anxiety below the surface. Your creativity-inducing biochemical processes shut down; your body deteriorates; the forces of evil (perhaps the devil himself) destroy you. An acceptable primitive response—like beatin' the tar out of something—can reopen the treasure chest. You'll still be angry, but you will have reversed the harmful effects on your nervous system.

Practice belly breathing for specific stressful events. Breathe slowly and deeply from the gut, twenty or more times. As your breath slows, your mind slows, and you become still. Also, rehearse controlled breathing: inhale deeply counting to five slowly, hold your breath for a few seconds, then let it out gently counting backwards. Much of the body's loss of control from stress follows autonomic (unthinking) reactions. Controlled breathing—taking away the automatic power of the central nervous system—can confuse the brain and reverse some stress. Many mystics proclaim that awareness of breathing comprises the most important part of any presentmindedness.

Prayer meditation also fools the autonomic nervous system and unwinds stress. Intensely focusing your awareness lulls you into a peaceful state reducing the hormone-induced sensations of respiration, heart rate, and muscle tension—all associated with stress. Also your blood lactate (a stress initiator) lowers, and your relaxing brain alpha waves increase. Transcendental Meditation teachers believe it takes a personal guru to teach meditation. Most mystics say otherwise.

When you first begin to meditate or indulge in lengthy prayer, mind chatter may overwhelm you. That's good. With a quiet mind you can see how much babble goes on in the subconscious all the time—preventing creativity. While meditating (or sleeping) the subconscious releases all this garble as the body eliminates stress toxins that have accumulated during the day. Let thoughts enter your mind and leave. Just don't get attached to them. The time between thoughts becomes the food for the soul. You'll eventually get it. The "nonthink" time will give you a whole new grasp on life. I heard a mystic say that it's impossible for a person to experience anxiety if he meditates or prays daily.

It helps me to "dump" my anxieties onto paper before I meditate. I unthinkingly write out all my mind chatter. Then I may make get-back-to-you-later appointments on my calendar. This little trick gives me enough present-mindedness to meditate and to gain even more present-mindedness.

When I first began, I could not meditate through lengthy praying until I practiced in the middle of a long vacation. Once I learned how, I can now do it most any time.

You can become more creative without meditating. With meditation you can become extraordinarily more creative.

Try "thought stopping." When junk starts getting to you, just yell to yourself, "NO! STOP!" The shock can trick your brain to back off. Concentrate on your breathing to bring back your presentmindedness. Here's another amusement: practice visualizing the world's most relaxing image. For me it's sitting on a creek bank fishing at a place no one else knows about. At times you can force this image to replace a troublesome thought. (Sometimes you can't, and anxiety just overcomes you. When this happens to me, I schedule "different stuff" and don't worry about being an uncreative meathead for a period.)

Leave no stress unattended. Eliminate the situation, or trick the brain's biochemical processes—especially with humor.

CHAPTER 8

Fighting Back

Enjoy the mental tricks that enable you to "float above it all."

Don't send negative messages to your subconscious, or let anyone else. Even better: fix what's causing your anxiety. Just do it.

Consider this. If you could have one big wish, what would it be? Quit this job, leave this creep, move back to Pittsburgh? If this one wish "belongs to you," it will probably happen anyway, so why not do it now? Heeding the obvious can relieve stress and open your creative life. Most of us have more regrets from what we didn't do than from what we did do.

Creative people become slightly more organized than others, not as an end in itself, but as a means to an end: to reduce stress. All of those who also implement their ideas well plan perpetually; they look into the future to schedule incubation and contemplative time. None of them let stress about the future cloud their surrendering and incubation. For example, if I wake at night feeling uneasy, I get up and put a note on my calendar. I make an appointment with myself to be concerned later.

Try to remember what Mark Twain said: "I'm an old man and have known a great many troubles—but most of them never happened." Realizing his wisdom, try practicing "attending to the work at hand," staying in the present, achieving your Zen. How? By thought stopping, by prioritizing lists, by going to new surroundings, by doing "different stuff," by scheduling reminders on your calendar.

Many of us have become driven people. Someone conditioned us—usually incorrectly—to believe we could do anything, and in large quantities. Making appointments with yourself enables you not to worry about what you're *not* doing at the moment. The famous Zen saying applies: "When I eat, I eat; when I sleep, I sleep." Baseball great Yogi Berra once made a Zen statement: "How could anybody hit the ball worrying about where it's going, or why he missed the last pitch?"

This concept of presentmindedness bothers some pragmatic people, but only because they do not understand the relationship to time that "practical" creative people have achieved. The rigid-minded have often been turned off by spaced-out cult followers. Creatively "attending to the work at hand"—not being bothered by the past or the future—comes from the suggestions in this book, mostly relating to eliminating guilt and anxiety. The guidance here differs from the live-one-day-at-a-time preaching to the gullible you may hear in some commune or from jewelry-laced TV evangelists. The naive crowd under the influence of a don't-worry-about-a-thing-just-send-your-money-to-me authority figure may achieve presentmindedness, but their subconscious may remain "unenriched."

(If so, they'll end up broke and disappointed later.) Successful people plan extensively and learn from mistakes; they discover how to psychologically set aside the past and the future when it's time to be creative. That does not mean they'll never have to deal with the future, only that they do not let it stress them right now. They've learned how to create "space for themselves."

Have you noticed how you feel great some days when you leave work, and on other days you're an uninspired mush-brain? A reason exists you may not have identified. On a note pad outside of work designate two pages for recording each day's activities. Leave one place for "up" days, another for "downers." After six weeks you'll see a trend. You may find that only a few job duties foul all days (like one hair in the salad ruining the entire meal). You may be able to concentrate these activities into just two stinking weekdays, leaving the rest for cheer and possible creativity. It sounds trivial, but it works.

Having a life's plan can also relieve anxiety. You no longer need to deal with the stress of "why am I doing this?" or "how am I doing?" You'll never see anyone become successful doing something he isn't passionate about. We talk of the delight of a good career, but pure toil makes up fifty percent of any job. To be successful, you need to love the drudgery too. Prosperous people like to do what lesser souls don't want to do. It's just that simple. You can't hang in there long enough if your job doesn't fit your life's purpose, if you haven't made the connection. When I meet creative, thriving superstars, I'm always amazed at how surprised they become when others make a big deal about their accomplishments. To them, serving their life's purpose through their job efforts seems to be natural and fun. If a task is enjoyable to you, you may be creative at it. If it's not, you probably won't. You will never find a way to continue doing it well with less effort, nor a way not to have to do it at all.

Here's another stress reducer: sometimes as part of your incubation process on important issues, try to develop an early viable alternative while not getting attached to it. As you begin to incubate further, set this "at-least-acceptable" option aside—with a real warm feeling void of stress. You know you have an alternative that would work if it had to. Freed from stress, the treasure chest opens and more alternatives flow. As an example, I often give sales presentations upon which a half-year's pay depends. If I screw up, I must live cheaper next year. As soon as I get the meeting date, I start all the enrichment and incubation recommendations of this book. I especially put reminders on my calendar so deadlines never sneak up. But I need more to keep stress away. Even though companies and consulting jobs differ, I first work up a draft spiel using old outlines and overheads. I set it aside with confidence—just in case.

Negative words stir up a ricochet of unpredictable emotions, closing your and others' treasure chests. Through practice, delete the following judgmental words and phrases from your vocabulary: "should," "must," "ought to," "have to," "deserve," "owe," "when are you...?" Stay away from people who use this kind of language. Sticks and stones *will* break your bones. Words *will* crash your spirit. Also alert your spouse and friends to help. My wife says, "Stop! Please," when I use this kind of negative language. Psychiatrists tell us that most destructive thoughts and behavior include such words. They all thrust some sort of overattachment or ego struggle onto someone—probably ourselves.

Judgment, on rare occasions, may have its place. But it doesn't mix with creativity—ever. This principle applies whether the judgment is directed toward yourself or toward others. Creativity involves an unleashing; judgment, on the other hand, limits the possibilities. Being judgmental puts others' (and your own) subconscious on the tightened defensive. As a result, associates often revert to creativity-killing excuse-making. Their energy drains—right out on the floor for the cat to lick up. (And the cat has no use for it.

Here's one of the hardest bits of advice to follow: to grasp true creativity, practice "being ordinary." Buddhist mystics call this unleashing "the wisdom of ordinariness." Uptight big shots seldom trigger their creative juices. The ego—more than anything else—closes the treasure chest. "But what will so-and-so think?" remains the question you want to avoid when you need to be innovative. Don't let others run your life at the very times you need to be the most creative. A trifling few environments still exist in which you can "keep your nose clean, bootlick a little," be seen working hard, play the game, look right, and do quite well. In the go-go decades of the past, when more advancement opportunities existed, it was often possible to "be a success, but not be successful." You could impress the boss—even by cheating others—and not have to hang around long enough in one place to get caught. But today more situations exist where creativity pays bigger dividends, and where everyone can detect a scheming, professional ladder-climber like a foul cat-box odor. You will need to dampen your ego to let the treasure chest open enough to work in these environments. My guess is that if you made it to this page, that's what you want. Creativity begins to flourish only when you learn to be unpretentious (not to mention the fact that people like you better and talk to you more honestly, so you'll learn more).

To advance your own interests, be ordinary.

A mystic once said that most grief comes from an attempt to prove a false sense of identity, usually based on a desire to be applauded and admired. Often we don't understand the march and the music because we think we *have* to be the drum major. This ego overattachment closes our treasure chests and makes us less likely to march and play well enough ever to become the drum major—assuming that's part of our life's purpose. (And there will always be others who are eager to help us fail).

Pretentiousness went out of vogue decades ago. (I think it happened at 2:13 P.M., March 3, 1965.) Being unpretentious may take far-reaching effort. A large part of the college curriculum, especially in business and engineering schools, involves professional "grooming." MBAs—especially those of you from top schools—take a look at yourself. Important people may be avoiding you because of your arrogance. Remember: "Conceit is God's gift to little men." It isn't profitable to be Mr. Big Shot.

With nothing to prove, you become a liberated person achieving new freedom because you don't have to demonstrate your intelligence. For the first time you learn how to listen creatively, to see connections others miss. Your treasure chest opens. You will realize that you can accomplish almost anything if you are willing to let others share the credit, and they will return the favor in most cases.

Being "ordinary" can also reduce biochemical brain damage and the creativity-kill resulting from anger. It's almost impossible to get enraged with someone when you perceive yourself as ordinary. Most hostility comes when someone challenges your haughty image of yourself. When you perceive yourself as an "ordinary" guy—with no image to protect—you can maintain your cool and keep the innovative juices flowing. (You can dish out deserved, creative revenge to disgusting scoundrels later. You know what they say about revenge being better served cold. On the other hand, if you've tapped into the magic, you'll probably decide later that the bum isn't worth the effort. A mystical friend of mine once said that scoundrels arrived on earth to show the rest of us how "not to be." Just avoid them.)

Fear of potential repercussions from the boss also smothers creativity. Being ordinary may even help here. Why threaten your boss with a conceited, threatening demeanor? It just isn't worth it.

Never close your treasure chest by taking an inflexible personal stand and staking your reputation on an issue that can be tested with data or facts. The ego closes the subconscious to further alternatives. An I-told-you-so attitude or a boastful personality also makes you an uncreative outcast. The subsequent bounce of emotions may close your treasure chest even further.

Until recently I did not understand a statement by the Mystic of all mystics: "The meek shall inherit the earth." Now I do. The world will become, or has already become, so complex and demanding that only the meek—the non-egotistical, "ordinary" people—will be able to keep their treasure chests open long enough to muster enough creativity to accomplish anything important. As we have noted, pretentiousness has gone out of vogue as we move into the new millennium.

Being ordinary remains difficult because of the mind chatter: "Be important, make your parents happy, earn accolades, win, live in the right neighborhood, be better than others." None of this mumbled gibberish exists in a true life's purpose. The blabbering **V**oice **O**f **J**udgment (VOJ) may help us at times with staying alive and not looking like a complete fool. But on other potentially calmer, creative days, we need to stomp egotistical, judgmental thoughts.

The mystic don Juan explained to Carlos Castaneda during one of their celebrated Mexican wilderness encounters that we have only a certain amount of psychic energy. The difference between life, as a consequence of biological forces, and the act of being alive, as a matter of deep-meaning cognization, involves releasing the energy we now use to maintain our image of importance. Lose this ego need and miraculous things begin to happen to you.

Part of the widespread spiritual movement involves the transition of society toward this new spiritualism. I heard one mystic call it "an evolutionary thrust toward a higher level of consciousness for all humanity." We see a religious movement outside, and within, the Church. But new-spiritualism thinkers usually avoid fire-and-brimstone preachers. I believe they know what an old, mystical preacher once told me: "Those who worship God from fear would follow the devil too, if he were to appear." At a worldly level, guilt, fear, and anxiety close the subconscious, preventing creativity and further learning. This diminishes spirituality and material accomplishments.

Modern thinkers search for a better understanding of what the subconscious has known all along: everything in the universe connects. All bad deeds get punished; all good deeds get rewarded. Every action becomes pregnant with worldly consequences entering the karma. The yin and yang always balance. On the other hand, any new-spiritualism folk believe that someday everyone goes to the same heaven (which may be in another dimension right here in our midst). They also sense the interconnectedness of all things—the collective unconscious of the human species. (The profound knowledge part of the management teachings of Edwards Deming covers this topic well. See REFERENCES, Fellers, *Why Things Go Wrong.*)

At first exposure I started to judge these new avenues of thought, but then extinguished my VOJ. Judgmental behavior of any sort closes my creativity and access to higher thinking. Remembering the biblical warning about casting the first stone, I kept on investigating the mystical experiences of others—whether religious, in a Western sense, or not. I believe it is better to learn what is probable (possible) about important matters than it is to be certain about trivial ones.

"Curiosity killed the cat." We all heard this adage in childhood, and we need to forget it as adults. The VOJ dampens curiosity, creativity's best friend. Excessive paperwork and rules—often the product of someone's VOJ—destroy creativity, not to mention wasting time. (The same applies to the expensive white sofa in the children's play room.) All rules or paperwork requirements, even the necessary ones, have a down side. Options get limited, curiosity wanes, creativity suffers. Feelings are affected, and enthusiasm is stifled. Look for ways to simplify your work life. While you're at it, simplify your entire life.

When you feel miserable and don't know why, it's likely your VOJ, or more specifically your parents' voices recorded in your brain before you were old enough to make value judgments, before you knew enough to discard the warnings that didn't apply any more. (Society attacks early when the individual remains helpless.) We often internalize trite sayings like, "Eat everything on your plate," or, "Don't talk to strangers." Hours spent analyzing your belief system from childhood will be well spent.

Pablo Picasso said, "Every act of creation is first an act of destruction." The VOJ needs to be set aside before wisdom can freely flow from the subconscious to release creativity.

Learn to control all judgmental thoughts and behavior.

Let's end this chapter with a review and some suggestions on how to help slay your VOJ:

Don't "act your age" unless you have to.

Always be curious. "Why's that?" remains a good question.

On planned creative days, at 6:00 A.M. unthinkingly write several pages of worrisome, nitpicking mind chatter. Set the list aside. This exercise tells your impressionable subconscious: "I've dealt with these distractions; ignore them."

Pay attention to your moods and the source of your melancholy.

Poke fun at the VOJ. It tricks you. Strike back.

Acknowledge life's roulette wheel. Uncertainty exists in almost every activity of life—driving to work, getting a job, finding a mate—or your department at work producing only 998 widgets, 1,000 being your "quota." Some occurrences just are not your fault.

Ask yourself these questions time and again:

"What's my VOJ saying here?" This question is especially important in response to fear, hurt, guilt, anger, sorrow. All grief is mental. When you experience such emotions, refer to your VOJ (the false self) as "it." Give it an identity separate from yourself, one you can set aside at will. Mystics say that it is impossible to change a false self. Powerful evil forces may have put it there, but you can condemn and ostracize it. In a way, you're "born again."

Practice thought stopping. Just say, "Stop it!" When you feel that thud in your midsection, let this signal you to get mad at your VOJ ("it"). Let your anger toward "it" replace the guilt and anxiety tied to your overattachments.

At this moment ask yourself these questions:

"How does what I'm doing fit with my life's purpose?"

"Am I acting like something I'm not (richer, interested in this job or the outcome, smarter, younger, more connected)?" Acting may not be so bad, but you can't be a creative whole person at the same time.

"Why does this guy/gal provoke me?"

"What stubbornness or bad decision am I hanging onto?"

"Who said that?" Was it your mother, father, or some other "authority figure"?

"What 'dumb' questions have I asked lately?"

"What did I observe or experience just for the fun of it today?"

"Who was my main teacher this week?"

"What did I learn from this experience?"

"What do I want to be doing this exact time next year?"

"Has this issue incubated long enough? Do I have enough alternatives to begin the verification process, to reality check, to outline an implementation strategy?"

These questions I can't answer for you, but you will know the answer to them, if you ask. Give ample lead time, and your subconscious will respond.

CHAPTER 9

Pulling It Together: Synthesis

Convert creative ideas into material and emotional successes.

Making the life transition toward creativity involves doing it all: enhancing learning, "whacking" the brain, surrendering and achieving presentmindedness to foster incubation, eliminating stress, and finding some extra time. Most importantly, to become mystically transformed, your subconscious must know your life's purpose, so you can be led into the correct experiences, so you can "ask, and you will receive." The parts work synergistically to yield $2 + 2 = 5$. Leave out something, and the results may be too small for you to remain motivated enough to continue your quest for wholeness and balance.

Drenching the subconscious with the facts of a particular situation (requiring creativity) may take hours or weeks, as may incubation on specific issues. Either based on a timetable you have given your subconscious, or at random times when answers just seep to the surface, you will get alternatives onto your personal note pad. At some point you will say, "It's time for the obvious: the analytical reality testing of the multiple alternatives—the verification." Creative ideas normally get born twice: once in the subconscious, and again out in the open where it's mostly "business as usual," when you verify, analyze, and compare.

What you already know will help you with verification—playing devil's advocate. We teach and nurture desk-top analysis well in schools, but be alert to visceral, gut feelings as you study alternatives. If it just doesn't feel right, it probably isn't, or at least something's wrong; there may be gaps in your knowledge. Let your mind be guided by reason, not bound by it. If time allows, go back to the drawing board for more alternatives. If not, go with your intuition.

Overly analytical people have often been conditioned to ignore their intuition. On the other hand, some other potentially creative people bypassed the important verification stage several times during impressionable periods early in their careers. Then they got burned by the bureaucracy or elders and eventually resigned themselves to a life of mediocrity. (Security needs likely kept them in their jobs or no-lives.) The insensitivity of their bosses and co-workers probably accentuated their downfall. It only takes one no in the lengthy chain of command to kill a new idea—and maybe a tender spirit too. Most administrators in the bureaucracy have the authority to say no; but almost no one has both the liberty and willingness to say yes. This situation can dampen a creative person's enthusiasm during his verification, causing him to mistakenly bypass the out-on-the-table analysis next time around.

As this book comes to a close, here is a good point to remember: dogmatic, rigid people and creative folk usually mix like desk librarians and giggling children. A first step may be to put some physical distance between you and the ogres while following my initial guidelines. (A two-week vacation may work. It will take four days of non-thinking to get you into a reflective mood.) Plan enough time and space so you'll begin to feel the magic. Once primed, the mystical forces in the universe will propel you forward. Then your subconscious will eventually provide the presentmindedness for you to find a new direction, or to accept your old one better so you can become more creative. When you grasp the magic, be careful: in the Republic of Mediocrity, genius is dangerous.

———————

Are you motivated to get creativity enhancement onto your desk? Practice! Then rehearse some more. It's difficult to make the self give up its strongholds except through practice. You will double your ability in several months. You will triple your enthusiasm within a half-year.

Place this book on your night stand. Glance at it calmly every evening for two weeks. Whisper to your sage after you lie down, "I am creative. I will become even more creative. Help me." Then drift away with confidence. Put a reminder on your calendar to re-read this book in two weeks. Plan several periods of "non-think" time for each of these weeks. Address your sage and intensely observe the children playing in the park.

Develop an action plan when you re-read.

Keep your copy of this book; you'll return to it every six months, until you feel the magic. Most people sense it during the second or third exposure—which you'll need before you lose sight of what you've learned.

Most management gimmicks—intended to get people to do something—have a half-life of about four months. But enhancing your creativity, and the enthusiasm it brings, will be with you forever. Tear out or copy the appendix. Review the steps within the next five minutes. Tape them on your wall to study daily until they become second nature—part of your permanent "enrichment."

Remember: presentmindedness, time management, sensory shock, stress reduction, and creativity enhancement go together. You will discover many useful things with your newfound enthusiasm. Good reading prepares the mind as a fun place to be—which is my goal for you. See you in two weeks when you experience this book again.

Remember: anxiety exists in the mind, as does peace. Trust and surrender.

ABOUT the AUTHOR: Dr. Gary Fellers consults with business clients to help them creatively improve quality and productivity. He also conducts seminars in creativity enhancement and the philosophy of Edwards Deming. Please write him in care of the publisher:

Pelican Publishing Company
P.O. Box 3110
Gretna, LA 70054-3110

Let him know if you want to be on his new-book or seminar notification computer list.

Appendix

THE TWELVE STEPS TO CREATIVITY

From the book *Creativity for Leaders* by Gary Fellers.

1.   Believe you can become more creative, and you will.

2.   Accept the existence of the mysterious subconscious—that incubates all previous experience and facts into creative ideas.

3.   With the goal of having more fun, create a life plan to "enrich" the subconscious.

4.   Patiently trust that answers will come.

5.   Trigger the subconscious by "visualizing" the desired outcome—in general terms. (It takes sixty seconds.)

6.   Surrender to your sage. Ask to be led to the correct experiences to achieve your life purpose.

7.   Write a life's purpose and prioritize around what's important.

8.   Make a game of saving time. Your most valuable resource deserves constant attention.

9.   Become a fanatic about presentmindedness:

attending to the work at hand. Put appointments on your calendar to think about distractions later.

10.   Leave no stress unattended. Eliminate the situation, or temporarily trick the brain's biochemical processes—especially with humor.

11.   To advance your interests, be ordinary.

12.   Stamp out all judgmental behavior and thoughts.

References

The worst thing about a new book is that it can keep you from reading old ones. This book is not intended to replace any of the references. You become a part of all you've read, so please continue. Entries marked with an asterisk (*) are mind-expanding crossover books.

Primary References

Fellers, Gary. *Why Things Go Wrong*. Gretna, LA: Pelican Publishing, 1994. (About Deming, fear, and more.)

Oech, Roger von. *A Whack on the Side of the Head*. New York: Warner Books, 1983.

Ray, Michael and Myres, Rochelle. *Creativity in Business*. New York: Doubleday, 1989.

Secondary References

Bono, Edward, de. *Six Thinking Hats*. Boston: Little, Brown, and Company, 1985.

*Boyles, Denis; Rose, Alan; and Wellikoff, Alan. *The Modern Man's Guide to Life.* New York: Perennial Library, Harper & Row, 1987. (A great book for women.)

Covey, Steven. *The 7 Habits of Successful People.* New York: Fireside Books, 1989. (See especially page 48.)

*Fellers, Gary. *Personal Agendas.* Forthcoming.

Gendlin, Eugene. *Focusing.* New York: Bantam New Age, 1981.

*Gleick, James. *Chaos.* New York: Penquin, 1987.

Gordon, Arthur. *A Touch of Wonder.* Old Tappan, NJ: Fleming H. Revell, 1974.

Levering, Robert. *A Great Place to Work.* New York, Boston: Random House, 1985.

McCoy, Doris Lee. *Megatraits.* Plano, TX: Woodware, 1988.

Naisbitt, John and Aburdene, Patricia. *Re-Inventing the Corporation.* New York: Warner Books, 1985. (See especially page 65).

Nathan, Ronald G.; Staats, Thomas E.; and Paul, J. *Instant Stress Relief.* New York: Ballantine Books, 1987.

*Pirsig, Robert. *Zen and the Art of Motorcycle Maintenance.* New York: Bantam Classics Spectra, 1984.

Rowan, Roy. *The Intuitive Manager.* New York: Berkley Books, 1986.

*Shim, Joe; Siegal, Joel; and Simon, Abraham. *The Vest-Pocket MBA.* New York: Prentice-Hall, 1986.

Winston, Stephanie. *The Organized Executive.* New York: Warner Books, 1985.

General References

Castaneda, Carlos. *The Art of Dreaming.* New York: Harper Perrenial, 1993.

Denning, Melita and Phillips, Osborne. *Psychic Self-Defense & Well Being.* St. Paul, MN: Llewellyn, 1993.

Howard, Vernon. *Mystic Path to Cosmic Power.* West Nyack, NY: Parker Publishing, 1967.

Kaku, Michio. *Hyperspace.* New York: Oxford University Press, 1990. (About parallel universes and beyond four dimensions.)

Leong, Kenneth. *The Zen Teachings of Jesus.* La Verne, TN: Publisher Resources, 1995.

McGee-Cooper, Ann. *You Don't Have to Go Home Exhausted.* New York: Bantam, 1992.

Morgan, Marlo. *Mutant Message Down Under.* New York: HarperCollins, 1994.

Potter, Beverly. *Finding a Path with a Heart.* Berkeley, CA: Ronin, 1995.

Rinpoche, Sogyal. *The Tibetan Book of Living and Dying.* San Francisco: Harper, 1994.

Ronner, John. *Do You Have a Guardian Angel?* Murfreesboro, TN: Mamre Press, 1985.

Talbot, Michael. *The Holographic Universe.* New York: Harper Perennial, 1992. (The ultimate "whack.")

Waller, James Lee. "Romance," *Old Songs in a New Cafe.* New York: Warner, 1994. (Read this if you never read anything else—especially pages 41-52.)